From the Bible-Tea...
CHARLES R.

D0729373

INSIGHT'S
ARCHAEOLOGY
Handbook

TEN KEY FINDS AND WHY THEY MATTER

INSIGHT FOR LIVING

INSIGHT'S ARCHAEOLOGY HANDBOOK
Ten Key Finds and Why They Matter

From the Bible-Teaching Ministry of Charles R. Swindoll

Charles R. Swindoll has devoted his life to the clear, practical teaching and application of God's Word and His grace. Chuck currently is the senior pastor of Stonebriar Community Church in Frisco, Texas, but his listening audience extends far beyond this local church body. As a leading program in Christian broadcasting, *Insight for Living* airs in major Christian radio markets around the world, reaching people groups in languages they can understand. Chuck's extensive writing ministry has also served the body of Christ worldwide, and his leadership as president and now chancellor of Dallas Theological Seminary has helped prepare and equip a new generation for ministry.

Published by IFL Publishing House, A Division of Insight for Living
Post Office Box 251007, Plano, Texas 75025-1007

The text was developed collaboratively by the Creative Ministries Department of Insight for Living. The contributing writers were:
John Adair, Th.M., Ph.D., Dallas Theological Seminary
Brianna Barrier Engeler, M.A., Biblical Studies, Dallas Theological Seminary
Derrick G. Jeter, Th.M., Dallas Theological Seminary
Wayne Stiles, Th.M., D.Min., Dallas Theological Seminary
Michael J. Svigel, Th.M., Ph.D., Dallas Theological Seminary

Editor in Chief: Cynthia Swindoll, President, Insight for Living
Executive Vice President: Wayne Stiles, Th.M., D.Min., Dallas Theological Seminary
Content Editor: Amy Snedaker, B.A., English, Rhodes College
Copy Editors: Jim Craft, M.A., English, Mississippi College
    Melanie Munnell, M.A., Humanities, The University of Texas at Dallas
Project Coordinator, Creative Ministries: Kim Gibbs, Trinity Valley Community College, 1991–1993
Proofreader: Paula McCoy, B.A., English, Texas A&M University - Commerce
Cover Designer: Amarilys Henderson, B.F.A., Illustration, Savannah College of Art and Design
Production Artists: Sharon D. Chandler, B.A., German, Texas Tech University
    Nancy Gustine, B.F.A., Advertising Art, University of North Texas
Images: Todd Bolen/BiblePlaces.com: cover, page 11 [inset], 14, 17, 22, 27, 30, 33, 36, 37, 41, 44, 49 [inset], 52, 62, 63, 69, 70, 75, 76, 78, 80, 85, 86
    Matt Floreen/www.mattfloreen.com: page 22 [enlargement]
    Rachel Floreen/www.mattfloreen.com: page 56
    Photos.com: page 11, 49, 65
    Zev Radovan/www.BibleLandPictures.com: page 11 [inset], 30, 46, 49 [inset], 88
    Wayne Stiles: cover, page 64, 67

ISBN: 978-1-57972-809-0
Printed in the United States of America

TABLE OF CONTENTS

APPENDIX

A NOTE FROM CHUCK SWINDOLL

I'll never forget my first year in seminary when I took a class called "Old Testament Introduction." I remember this quaint, little white-haired professor standing up front, who looked about 110 pounds, who blinked a lot, and who moved from side to side as he spoke. His name was Dr. Merrill Unger.

Before class, I had bought some of his books: Unger's *Bible Dictionary*, his *Introduction to the Old Testament*, and his *Archaeology and the Old Testament*. I thought, *Man, this is going to be great!* I assumed the class would be a simple survey. You know, we'd read a few verses of Genesis, see how they connected with Exodus and then Leviticus, and maybe peek into the prophets and look at what they taught. I expected an "introduction."

The very first session (I made a note of it), we were into subjects such as the uniqueness of the Old Testament, the theories of inspiration, the authorship of the Pentateuch, the canonical credentials, the Apocrypha, the pseudepigraphal texts, and the formation of the Masoretic text. We even glanced at the archaeological discovery of the Black Obelisk from Shalmaneser III . . .

"Wait!" Some young, frustrated theologian in the back shot up his hand. "Dr. Unger, I thought this was Old Testament *Introduction*!"

"Yes, it is," Dr. Unger replied. "That's why I'm keeping it simple."

When topics such as the Bible and archaeology come up, many Christians see the subjects as *anything* but simple. Most imagine only archaic languages, dusty digs, hot days, piles of rocks, and hard-to-spell terms like *archaeology*. In a word, they spell it: D-U-L-L!

But as I've discovered, we don't need to bury our heads, as some do, in the sands of apathy—or of fear. Some are scared to death that archaeology might unearth something that will destroy our faith! Recent popular fiction has played on such fears. But there's absolutely no reason to be afraid.

From the monumental discovery of the Dead Sea Scrolls, to the lesser-known inscription about Pontius Pilate, archaeology supports and affirms the names, places, and events the Bible proclaims as true. We have the archaeologist's spade to thank for these and many other significant finds.

In *Insight's Archaeology Handbook*, we have selected ten key discoveries and explained why they matter to you as a Christian. But rather than use archaic language and hard-to-spell words, we've taken care to avoid such clutter. Discussions that surround the Bible should make sense. To borrow from Dr. Unger's words, "That's why we're keeping it simple." But in our case, we really do mean *simple*!

I hope our archaeology handbook will equip you with a greater confidence in the Scriptures. For sure, it will encourage you on your spiritual journey.

Charles R. Swindoll

INSIGHT'S
ARCHAEOLOGY
Handbook

INTRODUCING THE *REAL* INDIANA JONES
Archaeologists and Their Work

by Brianna Barrier Engeler and Derrick G. Jeter

The hot wind turns cooler as the sun sets below the western horizon. On top of a mound of sand, men are working with pickaxes and shovels. They are digging because the archaeologist overseeing the work believes that the greatest discovery in all of history will be found in that very spot. Suddenly, sand turns to stone. Work stops for a moment—they've found a large stone block situated over a mysterious opening. Prying the stone free, the archaeologist drops a torch into the black abyss . . . and behold, they are standing on a temple that has been covered by the sands of time. This is it! In this very place history, tradition, and myth have come together—here is the discovery of all discoveries. One solitary archaeologist has solved the riddle. Wearing a leather jacket, sporting a fedora, and carrying a bullwhip, Indiana Jones is lowered into the temple. His prize? The Ark of the Covenant.

Steven Spielberg and Harrison Ford have made archaeologists into heroes and their work into the stuff of great adventure with movies such as *Raiders of the Lost Ark*. But as exciting as archaeological finds may be, the daily practice of archaeology doesn't look anything like what we see in the movies. In reality, archaeology is a long, slow, laborious endeavor not unlike putting together a three-dimensional puzzle after someone has thrown away the picture on the box and lost some of the pieces.

Defining Biblical Archaeology

Quite simply, archaeology is the "study of antiquity." [1] And it is far more than digging in the dirt and pulling out old objects. Putting together the puzzle of the past requires teamwork by experts in ancient languages, historians, geographers, artisans, geologists, ceramicists, biologists, and chemists. Each lends his or her expertise during an expedition, working to answer one question: What was this particular civilization like?

1

Biblical archaeology is unique when compared to other branches of archaeology because it provides a rich, cultural context for the history recorded in the Scriptures. Imagine what Pharaoh's opulent palace was like when Moses strode in to demand the freedom of the Hebrews. Picture the wooden vessels that Peter, James, and John might have used to ply their trade as fishermen on the Sea of Galilee. Envision the bustling city of Athens, filled with idols, when Paul debated the philosophers on Mars Hill. These and other stories come alive when historical and archaeological details come into play.

But how do archaeologists know what they are looking at when they find something? In fact, how do they even know where to dig?

The Tale of the Tell

In the early days, archaeology was no better than treasure hunting. However, the discipline has slowly developed into a scientific endeavor in which great care is given to preserve not only the artifacts but also an accurate record of what, when, and where an artifact is discovered. The ultimate goal is to understand what a particular artifact can tell us about an ancient civilization or event.

In pursuit of these goals, archaeologists often begin their work on what appear to be natural hillsides. However, these mounds — often fifty to one hundred feet high — are man-made.

Called *tells*, these mounds typically grew up from the successive destruction of buildings and the practice of rebuilding on the ruins of the previous settlement or city. Centuries of this cycle — destruction, rebuilding, destruction, rebuilding — produces stratification or "layers" that reveal much about the past occupants of the site.

So what caused the destruction of each of the various settlements? A common reason, especially during the biblical era, was the invasion of an enemy. Nations such as Assyria and Babylon were more interested in stripping all valuable resources from the cities they conquered than preserving their buildings. Other common causes of destruction were fires and earthquakes. Because buildings were usually made of mud bricks rather than stones, they were quite susceptible to natural catastrophes.

You may be wondering why ancient civilizations rebuilt on the rubble of destroyed ones. The primary answer is a practical one—people settled where water was readily available, especially in arid regions such as Palestine. Close proximity to trade routes, religious significance, military fortifications or defense strategy, and many other reasons also prompted this practice.

By the time of the Greek and Roman empires, the method of building on the ruins of a previous settlement largely ceased. New cities sprang up all over the ancient Near East and existing cities expanded as the population increased. Thus the buildings, monuments, and art of these eras were better preserved than those of earlier times. In fact, places like Rome, Athens, Corinth, Philippi, Ephesus, Petra, and Caesarea contain a treasure trove of archaeological sites and findings right at ground level where we can easily see them.

A Day on a Dig

Upon arriving at an excavation site, workers are instructed to report to the carefully mapped areas where digging will take place for the day. A supervising archaeologist oversees each section of the dig and directs the volunteer diggers. Field architects, photographers, artists, and ceramicists map, draw, and record the details of the dig. When an artifact is found, other specialists may be called in to evaluate it.[2]

Using large and small pickaxes, trowels, brushes, baskets, plumb lines, tape measures and, in some cases, sophisticated electronic equipment, tells are typically excavated in numbered squares measuring five to ten meters (approximately sixteen to thirty-two feet). The perimeters of each square, or *balks*, are left untouched because the interior faces of each balk usually reveal the varying strata or occupational layers of the tell. They also allow archaeologists and the work crew to move around the dig site without disturbing other excavation areas. As artifacts are uncovered, exact measurements record the placement of the find within the square. These measurements are then plotted on the field architect's drawing. And before the artifact is removed, it is photographed from many angles. Once carefully removed, the artifact is tagged with the square number and stratification level information, placed in a container, and taken to a field house for cleaning and evaluation.[3]

The Burden of Proof

Archaeology solves many riddles about ancient civilizations. But it cannot solve the mystery of faith. Though it can and does give credibility to various historical details and events mentioned in the Bible, deepening our understanding of the Scriptures, archaeology cannot scientifically *prove* the fundamentals of our faith. Nor does it intend to.

As you read and study these ten significant finds, rejoice in the evidence of the past that God has allowed us to uncover. Be encouraged by the historical accuracy of the Bible. But please keep in mind Paul's words: "Faith comes from hearing, and hearing by the word of Christ" (Romans 10:17).

ARCHAEOLOGY IN THE CONTEXT OF HISTORY

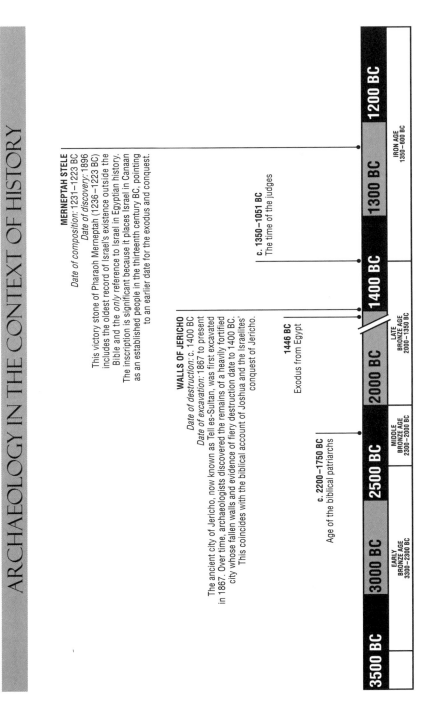

MERNEPTAH STELE

Date of composition: 1231–1223 BC
Date of discovery: 1896

This victory stone of Pharaoh Merneptah (1236–1223 BC) includes the oldest record of Israel's existence outside the Bible and the *only* reference to Israel in Egyptian history. The inscription is significant because it places Israel in Canaan as an established people in the thirteenth century BC, pointing to an earlier date for the exodus and conquest.

WALLS OF JERICHO

Date of destruction: c. 1400 BC
Date of excavation: 1867 to present

The ancient city of Jericho, now known as Tell es-Sultan, was first excavated in 1867. Over time, archaeologists discovered the remains of a heavily fortified city whose fallen walls and evidence of fiery destruction date to 1400 BC. This coincides with the biblical account of Joshua and the Israelites' conquest of Jericho.

1446 BC
Exodus from Egypt

c. 2200–1750 BC
Age of the biblical patriarchs

c. 1350–1051 BC
The time of the judges

3500 BC	3000 BC	2500 BC	2000 BC	1400 BC	1300 BC	1200 BC
	EARLY BRONZE AGE 3300–2300 BC	MIDDLE BRONZE AGE 2300–2000 BC		LATE BRONZE AGE 2000–1350 BC	IRON AGE 1350–600 BC	

ARCHAEOLOGY IN THE CONTEXT OF HISTORY

DAN STELE AND HIGH PLACE
Date of origin: c. 900–800 BC
Date of discovery: 1966 (High Place);
July 1993 and June 1994 (Stele, found in two pieces)

The High Place at Dan represented part of King Jeroboam's attempt to dissuade the Israelites from worshiping in Jerusalem under the dominion of David's House. The Dan Stele, originally an Aramean boast of victory over Israel, contains the first extrabiblical reference to the historical existence of the "House of David."

KETEF HINNOM AMULETS
Date of origin: c. 600 BC
Date of discovery: 1979

The Ketef Hinnom Amulets are tiny silver scrolls inscribed with the priestly benediction of Numbers 6:24–26. These amulets contain the earliest lines of written Scripture that have been found to date, predating the Dead Sea Scrolls by four hundred years. They also include the oldest form of the divine name, YHWH (Yahweh).

HEZEKIAH'S TUNNEL
Date of construction: 701 BC
Date of discovery: 1837

Hezekiah's Tunnel channels water from the Gihon Spring outside Jerusalem's walls to the Pool of Siloam, located inside the walls. Near the Siloam end of the tunnel, the workers carved the Siloam Inscription, describing the process of tunneling through solid rock.

c. 1051–1011 BC
King Saul reigned

c. 1011–971 BC
King David reigned

c. 970–931 BC
King Solomon reigned

722 BC
Fall of the northern kingdom

586 BC
Fall of Jerusalem

c. 538–432 BC
Jews return to Jerusalem

516 BC
Rebuilding of temple is completed

1100 BC	1000 BC	900 BC	800 BC	700 BC	600 BC	500 BC

IRON AGE
1350–600 BC

BABYLONIAN AND PERSIAN PERIOD
600–332 BC

ARCHAEOLOGY IN THE CONTEXT OF HISTORY

DEAD SEA SCROLLS
Date of composition: 250 BC – AD 70
Date of discovery: 1947
The Dead Sea Scrolls, arguably the most significant archaeological discovery of the twentieth century, reaffirm the integrity of our copies of Scripture, broaden our understanding of the Hebrew Bible by one thousand years, and better help us to appreciate the world in which Jesus lived.

356 – 323 BC
Alexander the Great lived

SEA OF GALILEE BOAT
Date of origin: 100 BC – AD 70
Date of discovery: 1986
The first-century boat discovered along the shore of the Sea of Galilee offers a unique glimpse at the type of vessel Jesus could have ridden in with His disciples. The preserved boat sits on display today at the Nof Ginnosaur Museum beside the Sea of Galilee.

POOL OF SILOAM
Date of construction: c. 50 BC
Date of discovery: 2004
The Pool of Siloam contained the water that flowed from the Gihon Spring through Hezekiah's Tunnel. It was also where Jesus sent the man born blind to wash and receive his sight (John 9).

27 BC – AD 14
Augustus Caesar reigned

THE TEMPLE MOUNT
Date of construction: c. 20 BC – AD 66
Date of discovery: Ongoing since 1968
Capped today by the glimmering Dome of the Rock, the Temple Mount is the most distinguishing mark of the Jerusalem cityscape. Nearly two thousand years after the destruction of the temple that once stood at the site of the current golden Islamic shrine, the massiveness and majesty of the Temple Mount still inspire awe.

THE PONTIUS PILATE INSCRIPTION
Date of origin: c. AD 26 – 36
Date of discovery: 1961
The Pontius Pilate Inscription, discovered during excavations in Caesarea by the Sea, is the earliest archaeological proof that Pontius Pilate was governor of Judea at the time of Jesus. This discovery confirms both biblical and historical accounts from the period and grounds Christianity's ancient creeds firmly in the bedrock of history.

5/4 BC
Birth of Jesus

AD 26 – 36
Pilate served as governor of Judea

AD 33*
Crucifixion and resurrection of Christ

AD 37
Paul converted to Christianity

AD 90 – 95
John exiled on Patmos

400 BC	300 BC	200 BC	100 BC	AD	100 AD	200 AD
BABYLONIAN AND PERSIAN PERIOD 600 – 332 BC		HELLENISTIC PERIOD 332 – 60 BC		ROMAN PERIOD 60 BC – AD 324		

*For more information, see Harold W. Hoehner, *Chronological Aspects of the Life of Christ* (Grand Rapids, Academic Books, 1977), 143.

FINDS IN ISRAEL

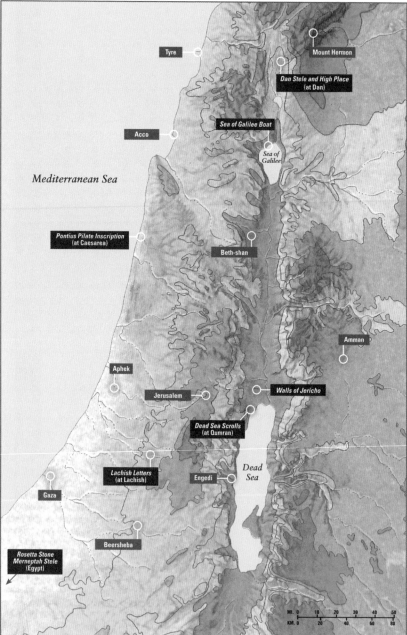

Tyre

Mount Hermon

Dan Stele and High Place
(at Dan)

Sea of Galilee Boat

Acco

Sea of
Galilee

Mediterranean Sea

Pontius Pilate Inscription
(at Caesarea)

Beth-shan

Amman

Aphek

Jerusalem

Walls of Jericho

Dead Sea Scrolls
(at Qumran)

Dead
Sea

Lachish Letters
(at Lachish)

Engedi

Gaza

Rosetta Stone
Merneptah Stele
(Egypt)

Beersheba

MI. 0   10   20   30   40   50
KM. 0   20   40   60   80

FINDS IN JERUSALEM

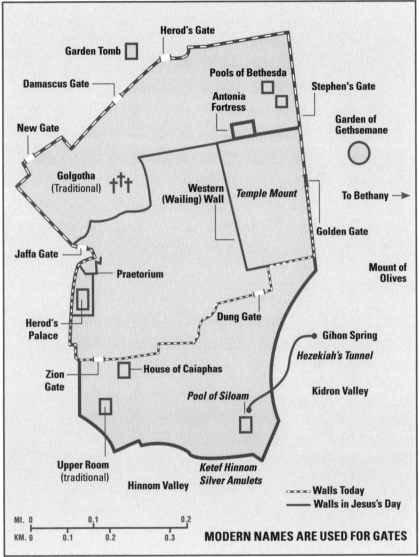

Herod's Gate

Garden Tomb

Damascus Gate

Pools of Bethesda

Antonia Fortress

Stephen's Gate

New Gate

Garden of Gethsemane

Golgotha (Traditional)

Western (Wailing) Wall

Temple Mount

To Bethany →

Golden Gate

Jaffa Gate

Praetorium

Mount of Olives

Herod's Palace

Dung Gate

Gihon Spring

Hezekiah's Tunnel

Zion Gate

House of Caiaphas

Kidron Valley

Pool of Siloam

Upper Room (traditional)

Hinnom Valley

Ketef Hinnom Silver Amulets

Walls Today
Walls in Jesus's Day

MI. 0   0.1   0.2
KM. 0   0.1   0.2   0.3   MODERN NAMES ARE USED FOR GATES

KEY
OLD TESTAMENT
Finds

THE WALLS OF JERICHO
Physical Evidence of Supernatural Intervention

by Brianna Barrier Engeler

Take a moment to imagine with me.

Everyone in town has heard about the Hebrews. Apparently, they escaped from Egypt with the help of an all-powerful God. And now, years later, they are marching into Canaan to conquer and destroy.

Your city is well-defended, with walls that tower into the sky. Jericho should be prepared for the worst siege an opposing army could muster. And yet . . . you feel the beginnings of fear curling deep in your belly. How powerful *is* their God?

They begin to march toward the city, and you secretly watch. Their priests are leading the way. What does that mean? Don't they understand the strategy of battle? Or are they truly led by a force you can't see? As they circle the city once, you hold your breath. What will happen?

When they finish circling the city, you're relieved and terrified at the same time. But day after day, they come back, walking around the city and then retreating. Your friends and neighbors begin to relax, assuming that their fears are unfounded. You, however, aren't so sure.

On the seventh day, the Israelites return. Around and around they go, and with each step your heart sinks further and further. Suddenly, you hear trumpet blasts and the earth begins to move beneath your feet. With an earsplitting crack, the famed walls of Jericho—fifty feet of solid protection—crumble to the ground. You hear the thudding feet and battle cries of the invaders. Women scream. Men fumble for the weapons they never thought they'd need. You try to run away, but there's nowhere to go. And on and on comes the sound of determined marching.

The terror. The horror. And the awe. Who could conquer the strongest city of all but a stronger God?

Jericho's Origins

Ancient Jericho, identified today as "Tell es-Sultan," is a large mound on the western outskirts of modern Jericho and may be one of the oldest settlements in the world. Some archaeologists date the city's beginnings to 7000 BC, based on the discovery of a Neolithic defense tower.[1]

Archaeologists believe that during the time of the biblical patriarchs (2000–1400 BC), Jericho was one of about twenty large urban centers in the land of Canaan. These towns were usually situated along the coast or where the water supply was abundant. And they were heavily fortified, suggesting a feudal culture in which cities fought one another as they tried to increase their holdings.[2]

Jericho, or "the city of palm trees" (Deuteronomy 34:3), was strategically positioned on the west side of the Jordan River in the eastern part of Canaan and controlled a vital water supply, the Ain es-Sultan spring.[3] Not surprisingly, Jericho's surviving cobbled streets, shops, storerooms, and living quarters reveal a bustling economy and culture.[4]

A panoramic view of modern Jericho, the "City of Palms"

The Biblical Account

While they were in the wilderness after the exodus, Moses told the Israelites that they would enter the Promised Land (Deuteronomy 9). God charged Joshua, as Moses's successor, with the task of leading His people to claim their inheritance (Joshua 1:2–9). Before attacking Jericho, Joshua sent two men to spy on the city. They entered the house of Rahab, a prostitute, and asked her to hide them from the king's men. In return, they promised that she and her family would be saved when the Israelites conquered the city (2:1–21).

After the spies returned, Joshua led the Israelites to Jericho. Once they reached the heavily fortified city, God directed His people to march around its walls once each day for six days and seven times on the seventh day (Joshua 6:3–4). They obeyed, and with a trumpet blast and a shout, the walls fell to the ground (6:20).

The Israelites rushed up into the city, destroying everyone and everything within it except for Rahab and her family. Then they burned the city to the ground, obeying the Lord's commands (6:20–24).

Excavations and Disagreements

In 1867, Sir Charles Warren began the earliest excavation of Tell es-Sultan. He sunk several trial shafts into the ground but did not find anything he deemed to be significant. Forty years later, archaeologists Ernst Sellin and Carl Watzinger traced the line of a wall surrounding Jericho.

The third official exploration of the city was led by John Garstang from 1930 to 1936. He uncovered masses of fallen mud bricks and two parallel walls surrounding the city. Combined with his discovery of a thick layer of ash, Garstang concluded that the city walls had been destroyed by an earthquake and a fire.

In order to date the destruction, Garstang studied Egyptian scarabs from tombs he opened around the tell. None of the scarabs were related to pharaohs who reigned later than Amenhotep III (approximately 1417–1379 BC).[5] He also found pottery consistent with the style used prior to 1400 BC but none of the painted pottery used in the following centuries. So Garstang concluded that the city fell about 1400 BC, a date which fits well with biblical chronology regarding the exodus.[6]

Archaeologist Kathleen Kenyon came to Tell es-Sultan in 1952 and challenged the dating of Garstang's finds. Her careful work confirmed that Jericho had been heavily fortified and that it had burned to the ground. However, she and her team believed that the city had been destroyed in 1550 BC by the Egyptians. Her work gave rise to a great debate over the date of Jericho's fall and, thus, the date of the exodus. (See also "The Merneptah Stele: How *Not* to Date the Exodus" on page 21.)

Recently, Dr. Bryant Wood meticulously reexamined Kenyon's excavation records. He concluded that she misread certain evidence and that John Garstang was correct—Jericho's walls fell about 1400 BC.[7]

Examining the Walls

Jericho was surrounded by an earthen embankment with a stone retaining wall at the base. This stone wall was approximately fifteen feet tall. Directly atop the stone stood a six-foot-thick, twenty-foot-high mud brick wall.[8] Another mud brick wall was erected at the top of the earthen embankment. The base of this inner wall was more than forty-five feet above ground level.[9]

Both Garstang and Kenyon found that the massive mud brick walls of Jericho had collapsed outward, falling down to rest over and against the outer stone retaining wall. The fallen bricks formed a makeshift ramp that allowed the Israelites easy access to the upper city—they simply climbed in.[10]

But according to Joshua 2:15, Rahab's house was built against one of Jericho's walls. How could her house have survived the Israelites' attack? Remarkably, Sellin and Watzinger discovered a small portion of the lower city wall that did not fall when all else was destroyed.[11] The section that remained standing was nearly eight feet high, with the houses built against it still intact.[12]

Garstang and Kenyon also found many storage jars filled with burned grain throughout the city. This discovery was highly unusual. Because grain was a valuable commodity in the ancient world, invaders usually plundered such resources.[13] However, consider the biblical account: Joshua and the Israelites burned everything in Jericho, taking nothing from the city, instead dedicating it as an offering to the Lord (Joshua 6:17).

In Light of the Evidence

When I was a child, one of my favorite songs to sing was "Joshua Fought the Battle of Jericho." I loved to do motions with the music, marching and blowing an imaginary trumpet. I'd much rather imagine myself on

Ruins of Jericho's mud brick retaining wall, possibly near the location of Rahab's house

the side of the Israelites and their God than that of the people inside the city. But in my childish celebrations of one of God's most awe-inspiring displays of power, I missed its historical reality. God promised His people the land of Canaan, and He made good on His promise.

He gave the land into their hands . . . and He left evidence behind for all to see.

DIG THIS!
EGYPTIAN PHARAOHS AND HEBREW HISTORY
*From Slaves to Judges**

PHARAOH	DATE OF RULE†	HEBREW HISTORY	DATE†	BIBLICAL PASSAGE
Ahmose	1570–1546	Slavery in Egypt	1570	Exodus 1:8, 11–14
Amenhotep I	1546–1526	Birth of Aaron, Moses's brother	1529	Exodus 7:7
Thutmose I	1526–1512	Hebrew infanticide and birth of Moses	1526	Exodus 1:15–16, 22; 2:1–2
Thutmose II	1512–1504			
Queen Hatshepsut	1504–1483			
Thutmose III	1504–1450	Moses kills an Egyptian and flees to Midian	1486	Exodus 2:11–15; Acts 7:23
Amenhotep II	1450–1425	Exodus of Hebrews from Egypt	1446	Exodus 7:7; 12:31–42
Thutmose IV	1425–1417			
Amenhotep III	1417–1379	Death of Moses at age 120 and conquest of Canaan	1406	Deuteronomy 34:7; Joshua
Amenhotep IV	1379–1362	Death of Joshua at age 110	1366	Joshua 24:29
Tutankhamen	1361–1352	Othniel's judgeship	1350	Judges 3:9
Ay	1352–1348			
Horemheb	1348–1320	Hebrew Baal worship	1340	Judges 3:7
Rameses I	1320–1318			
Seti I	1318–1304	Death of Othniel	1310	Judges 3:11
Rameses II	1304–1236	Ehud's judgeship	1275‡	Judges 3:15
Merneptah	1236–1223	Shamgar's judgeship	1230	Judges 3:31

Copyright © 2008 by Derrick G. Jeter. Used by permission.

*This chart was created using evidence compiled from Eugene H. Merrill, *Kingdom of Priests: A History of Old Testament Israel* (Grand Rapids: Baker Book House, 1987), 58 – 62, 146 – 48, 161 – 63. It should be kept in mind that precise dating is not possible, but a few years on either side of these dates doesn't disrupt the chronology of the biblical accounts as compared to the reigns of the pharaohs.
†All dates are BC. Dates represent years of births and deaths and the beginnings of events such as slavery in Egypt, the exodus from Egypt, the conquest of Canaan, and the rule of the judges.
‡Exact dating of Ehud's judgeship is difficult, but a range in the early quarter of the thirteenth century is not unreasonable: 1300 –1275 BC.

THE MERNEPTAH STELE
How Not to Date the Exodus

by Derrick G. Jeter

So let it be written. So let it be done."

Anyone who has watched Cecil B. DeMille's 1956 classic, *The Ten Commandments*, will remember these words. Though filled with biblical errors, DeMille's movie and Yul Brynner's magnificent portrayal have established in the public's mind that Rameses II (or Rameses the Great) was the pharaoh of the Hebrew exodus. But was he? Using biblical chronology and the evidence on a certain memorial stone (stele), we can determine who was pharaoh at the time of the exodus—just as it was written, just as it was done.

The Israel Stele, or Merneptah Stele as it's commonly known, is a black granite victory marker for Pharaoh Merneptah, who reigned from 1236 to 1223 BC.[1] The stele was discovered in Merneptah's mortuary temple in 1896.[2] The stone itself measures seven and one-half feet tall and has a striking relief carved into the top. Two images of the god Amon stand at the center. One faces left toward Merneptah and the goddess Mut. The other faces right toward Merneptah and the god Horus.[3] Below these images, written in hieroglyphics, are the details of Merneptah's early military triumphs, including his defeat of the Libyans and his invasion of Canaan, in which he engaged Israel in battle.[4]

What makes the Merneptah Stele fascinating is the reference to Israel during the Canaan campaign (1231 BC). At the bottom of the stone, in characteristic Egyptian bombast, Merneptah boasted of his conquests: "Canaan has been plundered in every evil way. . . . Israel is devastated, having no seed."[5] The inscription is significant because it's the earliest documentation of Israel besides the Bible and is the *only* account of Israel in Egyptian records. While these facts are important, the implications derived from them are momentous for biblical study.

The Merneptah Stele — the enlargement shows lines containing the reference to Israel

The Merneptah Stele inscription establishes Israel as a recognized people group in Canaan in the early 1200s BC. This is important because some scholars argue that the people of Israel at this time were nomads just entering the land to conquer it. That would put the date of the exodus in the late 1200s BC. (See "The Walls of Jericho: Physical Evidence of Supernatural Intervention" on page 13 for more information concerning the date of the Canaan conquest.) But if Israel was already established in the land, which the stele indicates by listing it alongside other established and conquered cities and states ("Askelon," "Gezer," and "Syria"[6]), then the date for the exodus must be earlier.

It's a tricky business using the Merneptah Stele to pinpoint a date for the conquest and exodus. Nevertheless, it is useful in setting certain chronological parameters.

Why Rameses II Was Not the Pharaoh of the Exodus

The stele argues convincingly against the "late date" theory (that the exodus occurred sometime around 1260 BC,[7] during the reign of Rameses II). If a late date is assumed, forty years are needed between the time Moses fled to Midian (Exodus 2:11–15; Acts 7:29–30) and his return to Egypt after the death of the pharaoh who sought to kill him (Exodus 2:23; 4:19–20). But the life of Rameses II doesn't fit this pattern. Though his reign was longer than forty years (1304–1236 BC), Rameses II is never identified as the pharaoh who died *before* the exodus but rather as the pharaoh *of* the exodus. If the latter is the case, either the biblical accounts of pharaoh's death, which prompted Moses's return, are incorrect or the scholars are wrong. If the former is the case and Rameses II was the pharaoh who died, that places the exodus sometime after 1236 BC and within the reign of Merneptah. Virtually all scholars view this possibility with contempt because an additional forty years are required for the wilderness wanderings (Numbers 14:27–35), dating the conquest of Canaan at 1196 BC, twenty-seven years *after* the reign of Merneptah.[8]

Therefore, the biblical record and the Merneptah Stele allow us to safely discard a "late date" theory for the exodus. But can we determine an "early date" for the exodus that squares with the biblical account and fits within the reign of another pharaoh? Happily, we can.

Why Amenhotep II Was the Pharaoh of the Exodus

First Kings 6:1 unambiguously states, "In the four hundred and eightieth year after the sons of Israel came out of the land of Egypt, in the fourth year of Solomon's reign over Israel, . . . he began to build the house of the Lord." Solomon's fourth year is well confirmed as 966 BC.[9] If the exodus occurred 480 years before, then it must have taken place in 1446 BC. This corresponds to the reign of Amenhotep II (1450–1425 BC).[10] (For more information, see the chart "Egyptian Pharaohs and Hebrew History: From Slaves to Judges" on page 19.)

Confirming an exodus date at roughly 1446 BC is also supported by Judges 11:15–27, in which Jephthah argued that the Ammonites had no ground for enmity against Israel because of their occupation of Canaan: "While Israel lived in [the land for] three hundred years, why did you not recover [it] within that time?" (Judges 11:26). Jephthah's judgeship was approximately 1100 BC. His message speaks of events just before the conquest of Canaan, placing a date for that event around 1406 BC and the exodus at 1446 BC.[11] So, in chronological terms, Amenhotep II is the best candidate as the exodus pharaoh. We also find interesting circumstantial evidence surrounding his reign that mirrors the biblical account.

So, then, who was the earlier pharaoh—the one from whom Moses fled? The Bible requires a forty-year time period before the death of this pharaoh allowed Moses to return to Egypt from Midian, so a pharaoh who reigned at least forty years is necessary. Thutmose III (1504–1450 BC) fits nicely. Moses killed an Egyptian at the age of forty and then fled to Midian (Acts 7:23–29). Assuming the biblical chronology is correct, this event transpired in 1486 BC.

Moreover, Exodus 12:29 says, "The Lord struck down all the first-born in the land of Egypt, [including] the firstborn of Pharaoh who sat on his throne." After Thutmose III, Amenhotep II rose to the throne, followed by his son Thutmose IV. But we know that Thutmose IV was not the eldest. He indicated in an inscription called the Dream Stele that Amenhotep's firstborn son died before ascending the throne.[12] This incident, and the fact that Amenhotep may have suffered a catastrophic military defeat late in his reign (compare Exodus 14:21–28), is a curious correlation with the biblical narrative.[13]

So Let It Be Written. So Let It Be Done.

The Merneptah Stele, along with the biblical record, rejects Rameses II or Merneptah as the pharaohs of the exodus. It points to an earlier time, an earlier pharaoh. Amenhotep II and 1446 BC fit the bill.

This should renew our confidence that the Bible is an actual account of God's activities in and through historical events and people, and that by His sovereignty He can even use pagan pharaohs like Merneptah to point us to the truth. So let it be written. So let it be done.

DIG THIS!

The Rosetta Stone: From Art to Eloquence

Strange-looking birds, bulls with disks on their heads, and flat, one-dimensional people—you've seen them carved or painted in stone: Egyptian hieroglyphs. Untrained eyes see beautiful artwork, nothing more. But to trained eyes, the fanciful shapes tell the history of an ancient civilization.

Hieroglyphs had always been thought of as merely pictographs, not an advanced language. However, in 1799, while Napoleon's troops were expanding the walls of a fort near the village of Rosetta, west of the Nile delta, they uncovered a large black stone, approximately four and one-half feet high by two and one-half feet wide.[1] Unknown at the time, this stone would provide the key to decoding the ancient language of the Egyptians.

The engravings on the Rosetta Stone are divided horizontally into three sections, each containing different writing styles. The top consists of fourteen lines of *hieroglyphs*, a word that is rendered from the Greek words meaning "sacred" and "carved in stone."[2] The middle is comprised of thirty-two lines of *demotic*, a common form of Egyptian script. The bottom contains fifty-four lines of Greek letters.[3] Each inscription depicts the same event: honor paid to Ptolemy V Epiphanes by Egyptian priests in 196 BC for his generous endowment to Egyptian temples, declaring him a god and pharaoh forever.[4]

Deciphering the Rosetta Stone baffled scholars for years. But then a bright, young French scholar, Jean-François Champollion, using his knowledge of the Greek and Coptic languages, decoded the hieroglyphs in 1822. Champollion realized that hieroglyphic symbols represented letters, ideas, and phonetic spellings.[5]

Because of Champollion's work in translating hieroglyphs, archaeologists and Egyptologists are now able to understand the eloquence of the beautiful artwork, increasing our knowledge of both ancient Egypt and the context of early biblical history.

The Rosetta Stone, including hieroglyphs, demotic, and Greek

KING DAVID VINDICATED

The Discovery of the Dan Stele and High Place

by Wayne Stiles

Walking around the archaeological site of "Tel Dan" in northern Israel felt like traipsing through the American northwest. Cool, green, and shady, the place looked to me like none of the rest of Israel. Uneven, rocky pathways and shaded trails encircle the ancient tell and crisscross the Dan Spring. The spring flows from the base of Mount Hermon and remains the longest and most important source of the Jordan River.

I paused to grin before a wooden sign painted in Hebrew: "Garden of Eden." It must have seemed that way to the tribe of Dan when they arrived.

After abandoning their God-given inheritance down south, the Israelite tribe of Dan migrated to this fertile area, also abandoning their worship of God. While the tabernacle remained at Shiloh, the Danites bowed before a graven image in their new digs up north. And of all people, the grandson of Moses served as priest (Judges 18:30 NIV).

Centuries later, King Jeroboam repeated the folly. The nation of Israel had divided into two parts. Now there were two nations, two kings, and two capitals — but still only one place God allowed for worship: Jerusalem. King Jeroboam felt that his northern kingdom of Israel was being threatened by the worship of God at Jerusalem, in the southern kingdom of Judah. Jeroboam feared "the kingdom will return to the house of David" (1 Kings 12:26).

The Dan Stele and the "House of David"

Navigating the cobblestones beneath my feet, I approached a large, rock wall that our guide told us represented a city gate from the time of Solomon's temple. Built in the ninth century BC, most likely by

Gateway to the ancient city of Dan, where the Dan Stele was discovered (in the foreground)

The Dan Stele—the enlargement indicates the Aramaic inscription, "House of David"

King Ahab, this Iron Age entrance served as one of a series of gates that fortified the Israelite city of Dan, now called "Tel Dan."

To my right, in the courtyard of the gate complex, I saw a sign that indicated the location of a significant discovery. There archaeologists had unearthed sections of a large, basalt stele — an ancient engraved stone — which boasted of an Aramean king's victory over Israel at Dan. The ninth and early-eighth centuries BC gave stage to a number of wars between the northern kingdom of Israel and its neighboring enemy, the expanding kingdom of Aram. Once the Arameans had conquered Dan, the king of Aram erected a victory stele to memorialize the event. Evidently, a subsequent Israelite king had smashed the stele and buried it outside the gate where I stood.

I remember seeing the actual Dan Stele in Jerusalem's Israel Museum. The inscription, written in Aramaic, most significantly mentions the Aramean king's victory over the "House of David." What's so significant about that? This phrase represents the first and only text outside of the Bible that refers to the "House of David," meaning to his family or dynasty. In fact, "Ever since the excavation of these fragments in 1993 and 1994, this Syrian reference to the 'house of David' has been extremely troublesome to a small group of liberal scholars ('minimalists') who deny the historicity of David."[1]

Prior to the Stele's composition, Jeroboam tried to dissuade the Israelites from returning to worship in Jerusalem by building an alternative place of worship in Dan (more on that below). Ironically, later Tel Dan actually served to *validate* the existence and importance of the "House of David" through the inscription discovered there, which dates to about one hundred years after David's death. An additional paradox arises when we realize that an *enemy* of the Hebrews inscribed the stone! In other words, the site that Jeroboam intended to challenge David's dynasty eventually ended up vindicating it. I love God's providential ironies.

Crowning Convenience

To try to restrain his people from worshiping in Jerusalem, Jeroboam made two golden calves and said, "It is too much for you to go up to Jerusalem; behold your gods, O Israel, that brought you up from the land of Egypt" (1 Kings 12:28). So, while Solomon's temple stood in Jerusalem, Jeroboam sanctioned the worship of a golden calf at a high place in Dan (12:26–30).

I approached a large, open area with tooled stones stacked in the arrangement of an altar. A modern, steel frame sat on top of the stone podium, indicating the original size and location of the horned altar once erected there. Nearly all archaeologists agree that this location represents the "high place" where Jeroboam set up his golden calf and offered sacrifices. I shook my head as I considered its implications.

Jeroboam appealed to the laziness of the human spirit and established an alternate and more convenient religious experience for his people. He set up one calf in Bethel, which sat as a roadblock on the way to Jerusalem. The other calf he set up here in Dan.

As I looked around at the area, with its lush springs, rivers, and shade trees, I understood why the Hebrews traveled even "as far as Dan" to worship (12:30). In the way of amenities, it had everything Jerusalem lacked. It was like worshiping in the verdant, tropical gardens of Hawaii.

In addition to offering a substitute temple, Jeroboam made substitute priests and a substitute feast as well. For Israel, worship became self-worship at the altars of convenience and recreation.

What Jeroboam pitched to Israel, the world and the Devil also solicit us: "It is too much for you to obey the Lord; try this alternative instead." Sin always provides us a convenient and appealing substitute—in other words, a counterfeit. But ease must never determine our spiritual priorities. Our relationship with the living God must remain a matter of obedience before convenience.[2]

The High Place of Tel Dan where Jeroboam erected a worship center, including an altar and a golden calf

DELIVER US FROM EVIL
The Story of Hezekiah's Tunnel

by John Adair

On marched the invading hordes. They came to exact judgment; they came for blood. For King Hezekiah of Judah, who had trusted the Lord and rebelled against the Assyrian oppressors (2 Kings 18:7), the consequences were grave. The Assyrian invasion now threatened to overthrow Hezekiah's cities, and with this would come terrifying kidnappings and killings and the violent upheaval of God's people from their Promised Land.

In 701 BC, Assyria's armies laid siege to fortified cities throughout Judah. In Jerusalem, King Hezekiah perceived the imminent danger and began to take action. First, he tried to buy off King Sennacherib of Assyria, paying him tribute (2 Kings 18:13–16). However, that proved ineffective when the King of Assyria sent emissaries and an army to Jerusalem, preparing for a fight.

As Sennacherib began to tighten his noose around Judah, Hezekiah rebuilt the wall around the city, added a second wall farther out, and increased the production of weapons and shields (2 Chronicles 32:5). But with the prospect of death closing in around them, Hezekiah needed a way to infuse life into a city filled with terrified inhabitants. How would he sustain a city under siege?

Constructing a Solution

Hezekiah's solution was ingenious. He blocked up the natural springs outside the city to ensure that the Assyrians would not benefit from having such a significant source in unlimited supply so nearby (2 Chronicles 32:3–4). And in the case of the Gihon Spring, Hezekiah not only blocked it from the Assyrians but redirected it into Jerusalem by means of a tunnel underneath the city (2 Kings 20:20; 2 Chronicles 32:30).

The path of Hezekiah's Tunnel, running under the City of David
[Above Insert] Entrance into the tunnel, just to the east of the city wall
[Below Insert] Steps into the Pool of Siloam, which held the water from the tunnel

To expedite the construction of "Hezekiah's Tunnel," two teams were dispatched—one to the east of the city at the Gihon Spring, the other to the southwest, inside the city walls just below the old city of David at what would become the Pool of Siloam. With iron-headed pickaxes, the men hewed away the stone. Night and day they worked, some men cutting stone away while others carried it out of the two tunnels. Miraculously, they met in the middle, in spite of a twisting route that must have been difficult to trace precisely.

Just inside the city walls at the Siloam end of the tunnel, some of the men carved an inscription into the stone wall detailing their work. This "Siloam Inscription," rediscovered in 1880 by a child playing in the tunnel, describes the workmen first hearing the voices of their fellow stonecutters in the next tunnel. They quickly turned their axes toward those voices and, with renewed energy, broke through the last few feet of stone. With the few remaining remnants of stone removed, the spring water flowed freely through the tunnel, spilling out inside the walls of Jerusalem at the Pool of Siloam.[1]

The Siloam Inscription, written in the Hebrew script of Hezekiah's day

Standing Strong in the Face of Oppression

Upon the commissioning and completion of this tunnel, which extends to just over one-third of a mile, Hezekiah provided a continual source of hope to his beleaguered citizens, even if it was only a trickle at times. The most powerful and destructive army in the known world was bearing down upon them, leaving the Israelites' future in doubt. Yet the constant supply of water surely strengthened their resolve. And they needed every possible edge, as their hopeful attitude was later tested by the haughty and contemptuous warnings offered by the Assyrian commander Rabshakeh, who had been sent by King Sennacherib to influence the people to surrender (2 Kings 18:17–35).

They refused, though the Assyrians certainly had shaken their courage. While the improvements helped matters, the long siege ahead of them and the lack of neighboring cities to provide assistance made clear the inherent weakness of their position from a military standpoint. Jerusalem had been left as an island amid a sea of Assyrian control. With nowhere left to turn, Hezekiah and his men sought the Lord through the prophet Isaiah. He told them to stand firm, for the Lord would surely deliver them from this menace (Isaiah 37:6–7). And deliver He did, when an angel killed 185,000 men in the Assyrian army, forcing their retreat from Judah (2 Kings 19:35–36).

Amazingly, a discovery called the Taylor Prism (named for the man who brought it to Britain in 1830 from Nineveh, the location of ancient Assyria's capital) describes Sennacherib's foray into Judah. This six-sided piece, made of baked clay, confirms a number of key details from the biblical account—namely, that Sennacherib did indeed invade Judah, that he conquered a great number of cities, that he trapped Hezekiah in Jerusalem ("like a bird in a cage"), and that Hezekiah paid him tribute. Consistent with the biblical account, the king makes no mention of actually conquering Jerusalem. (In the huge reliefs carved into the palace walls in Nineveh, the Assyrian king's great victory is over the city of Lachish.) Certainly, had Jerusalem and its king been conquered, that would have served as the great victory worth memorializing.[2] The Taylor

Prism preserves an additional account of this biblical event, and while there are differences between the two, the similarities are such that there can be no doubt they describe the same event.

Hezekiah's Tunnel Today

Hezekiah's Tunnel was an important achievement in Hezekiah's day, and it remains in use today. It funnels water into the Pool of Siloam, which, at least in modern times, has often been used for washing clothes. In 1838, Edward Robinson, a prominent American explorer, rediscovered the tunnel for those of us in the West, though it was well-known among those living in Jerusalem at the time. He measured it exactly (1,750 feet) and traced its S-shaped route to confirm the water's origins at the Gihon Spring.[3] Once the tunnel was explored and the silt cleared out, it could handle foot traffic. Now, though some areas of the tunnel are narrow, tour groups in Israel can walk through it and gain a sense of the scale of this impressive feat of workmanship.

Hezekiah's Tunnel remains a testimony to God's faithfulness to deliver His people in times of need. He used a number of means to accomplish this in the conflict between Israel and Assyria, but the tunnel continues to stand out as a tangible expression of God's life-giving power.

DIG THIS!
The Last Days of Judah: The Lachish Letters

Broken pieces of pottery buried in dirt mounds lie all over Israel, waiting to be discovered. One such discovery in the 1930s by a British team digging at the former Judean stronghold city of Lachish included some fascinating letters. Written in ink on clay, the eighteen letters or *ostraca* were updates from a Judean officer stationed at a military outpost addressed to his commander in Lachish. Some are unreadable, but at least two of the letters contain intriguing similarities with the biblical accounts of the final days of Judah during the Babylonian invasion that began in 597 BC—over one hundred years after Hezekiah.

Letter 3 describes an encounter with a Judean commander named Coniah, who passed through the outpost on his way to Egypt in an effort to procure military assistance from Pharaoh. The letter ends with a warning from an unnamed prophet.[1] This coincides with Jeremiah's warning to King Zedekiah against his false hope that Egypt would come to Judah's rescue when Babylon attacked (Jeremiah 37:6–8; Ezekiel 17:11–17).

Letter 4 appears to have been written in the final, desperate days of the garrison. The young officer notes, "We are watching for the beacon from Lachish, following the signals you, sir, gave, but we do not see Azekah."[2] These "signals" probably refer to smoke signals or bonfires that would have communicated warnings or assurances that the city was still standing. The fact that he was looking to these cities shows they were the last remaining during the fall of Judah. This confirms Jeremiah 34:7 in which the prophet notes that even as the Babylonians attacked Jerusalem, both Lachish and Azekah held out.

Gate into the city of Lachish, with a sign indicating where the letters were discovered

THE KETEF HINNOM AMULETS
Tiny Bits of History with Enormous Implications

by Brianna Barrier Engeler

W hen you see the word *tomb*, what immediately comes to mind? Feelings of sadness? Images of grieving families? A marble mausoleum or a six-foot-deep hole in the earth?

An archaeologist would probably answer that question quite differently. To a seasoned researcher, a tomb can be an intriguing treasure trove of information about the past.

A Window into Ancient Times

Tombs that date back to Old Testament times have been discovered all over Jerusalem and in the surrounding areas. One of the greatest concentrations of burial sites is in the Hinnom Valley, located just south and west of the Old City of Jerusalem.[1]

Tombs in those days consisted of a square room with three waist-high benches lining the chamber. Bodies were placed on these benches immediately after death, along with all sorts of burial gifts. Only the wealthiest families in Israel could afford a tomb quarried out of rock, so these gifts usually included jewelry, pottery of many kinds, perfumes, weapons, oil lamps, and more. After the corpse had decayed, the bones and gifts were collected and placed into a repository below the benches. Over time, these repositories filled with bones and objects from many generations.[2]

Most burial repositories were looted by grave robbers over the centuries, leaving precious few for archaeological study. However, the intact repositories that have been found contained a great number of priceless artifacts, shedding light on daily life in ages gone by.

A Remarkable Discovery

In 1979, Dr. Gabriel Barkay and his team began an expedition at Ketef Hinnom, a burial site just southwest of the Old City of Jerusalem. They focused on the excavation of several rock-hewn tombs. Most of the tombs had long ago been plundered. However, in one of the larger tombs Barkay's group uncovered a repository that was surprisingly untouched. Nearly a thousand objects were inside, from small pieces of pottery to metal arrowheads, from ivory pieces to jewelry.

The most important find of the dig proved to be two tiny strips of silver, tightly wound and resembling miniature scrolls. When the tiny scrolls were unrolled, they revealed carefully etched inscriptions containing a shortened version of the priestly blessing found in Numbers 6:24–26:

> "The LORD bless you, and keep you;
> The LORD make His face shine on you,
>   And be gracious to you;
> The LORD lift up His countenance on you,
>   And give you peace."

Dr. Gabriel Barkay at the Ketef Hinnom repository / tombs

The larger of the "Ketef Hinnom Amulets," as they came to be called, is about four inches long and one inch wide when unrolled. The other is about an inch and a half long and half an inch wide. Using archaeological and paleographic evidence, Dr. Barkay dated them to the late seventh or early sixth century BC, nearly four hundred years earlier than the Dead Sea Scrolls. (See "Resurrecting Scripture: The Discovery of the Dead Sea Scrolls" on page 61.) Based on Dr. Barkay's conclusion, the amulets are the earliest written lines of Scripture found to date.[3]

A Controversial Inscription

The dating of the Ketef Hinnom Amulets was quickly questioned, partly because reading the inscriptions proved to be exceedingly difficult. The silver was corroded in areas, and many of the words were partially missing. Some thought that the inscriptions were written in an "archaistic" rather than a truly "archaic" script—making them look older than they actually were. Other scholars questioned the find as it related to a broader controversy among historical circles.

The debate taps into the origin and authenticity of Scripture. The passage of Scripture inscribed on the amulets is part of the Torah, the first five books of the Bible. Traditional scholarship holds to the ancient origins of these texts, first passed down through oral tradition, then written and compiled into the basic form that exists today. Others argue that the Bible was a more recent invention, written by those who took control of Palestine in the late fourth century BC. These scholars believe that the invaders sought to create their own history and thus lay claim to the land.[4] However, if the dating of the Ketef Hinnom Amulets was confirmed to be near 600 BC, it would corroborate the Bible's claim of its own antiquity.

The controversy surrounding the amulets continued unabated until 2003, when a group of researchers from the University of Southern California teamed up with the West Semitic Research Project to reexamine the scrolls using new photographic and computer-imaging techniques. Innovative lighting revealed the inscriptions in greater detail. Computer imagery reconstructed missing words. And skilled linguists compared the writing style with other writings from the seventh century BC.

The researchers conclusively dated the strips as coming from the period just before the destruction of the first temple in 586 BCE.[5]

Thus the priestly benediction of Numbers 6:24–26 carried on the Ketef Hinnom Amulets is the earliest written biblical passage discovered to date. The Hebrew name of the Lord, YHWH (Yahweh), also appears in writing for the first time.

The Importance of Amulets

So what was the purpose of wearing the amulets? And why were they placed in a tomb?

In the ancient world, amulets were charms elaborately inscribed with religious symbols or special incantations. Worn around the neck as jewelry, they were meant to protect the wearer from evil or bodily harm.[6] Due to their size and shape, it is likely that the Ketef Hinnom Amulets were designed for this purpose. Part of the inscription on the smaller artifact also indicates that the scrolls were worn as amulets. It reads, "May h[e]/sh[e] be blessed by YHWH, the warrior [or: helper], and the rebuker of [E]vil."[7] This phrase is found in later amulets and prayers associated with ancient Israel.[8]

Later Jewish traditions quoted the priestly blessing of Numbers 6:24–26 as part of burial or funeral ceremonies, so the "discovery of the plaques in the burial repository suggests that they served to bless the deceased person's journey to Sheol, the netherworld or abode of the dead."[9]

The smaller of the Ketef Hinnom silver amulets (not actual size)

A Reminder of Faith

As I write this, I keep fingering the tiny cross pendant that I often wear around my neck. It's not an amulet; I don't expect it to offer me some sort of magical protection. The cross is a simple reminder of my faith in Jesus Christ.

I can't help but wonder about the person who wore the silver amulets so many centuries ago. Was she a young woman like me? Did she touch them throughout the day as she prayed? Were they a source of comfort for her as she contemplated Yahweh, the God of her forefathers? Did they mean so much to her that she asked that they be buried with her someday?

For just a moment, contemplate the words she held so close to her heart.

> "May the LORD bless you and protect you.
> May the LORD smile on you and be gracious to you.
> May the LORD show you his favor and give you his peace."
> (Numbers 6:24–26 NLT)

May He grant you peace.

KEY
NEW TESTAMENT
Finds

A LOOK AT THE *REAL* INDIANA JONES
Interviews with Archaeologist Bryant Wood and Professor Todd Bolen

by Derrick G. Jeter

As a character in a series of movies, Indiana Jones has become almost mythical in stature. Not only does he travel to exotic locations in search of history-changing archaeological artifacts—that belong in museums for the benefit of humanity—he outwits the bad guys who wish to use these artifacts for their own evil ends. An expert in biblical, Inca, and medieval history, myth, and archaeology, Indiana Jones is a crackerjack with a bullwhip and fearless in his pursuit of archaeological treasures—fearless, that is, unless snakes are involved.

Because of these movies we've come to think of archaeologists as heroic, engaged in derring-do, and always getting the girl. Our interviews with two real-life Indiana Joneses reveal a different picture of the popular figure cut by Harrison Ford.

After a career as a mechanical engineer, Dr. Bryant Wood was called by the Lord into professional archaeology. Earning his Ph.D. in Syro-Palestinia archaeology from the University of Toronto, Dr. Wood now serves with the Associates of Biblical Research in Akron, Pennsylvania. Although Professor Todd Bolen isn't a professional archaeologist, he is a biblical scholar, having lived and taught in Israel for more than eleven years, with extensive experience in leading students on archaeological excavations.

We caught up with both men and asked them questions to help us better understand what archaeologists actually do and why it's important to the Christian faith.

Bryant Wood at Jericho, pointing to fallen mud bricks

How did you become an archaeologist?

Bryant Wood (BW): My interest in biblical archaeology began when my mother-in-law gave me a book on archaeology and the Bible the Christmas after I graduated from Syracuse University.

What interests you most about archaeology?

Todd Bolen (TB): Archaeology is fascinating because it gives us another source for the ancient world. Literary texts, including the Bible, are limited in the amount of information that they provide, but archaeology can tell us more about the way that people lived. Archaeology sometimes reveals the "other side of the story"; for instance, the Moabite Stone gives the enemy's [the Moabites'] perspective of the events recorded in 2 Kings 3, and the archaeological material from Qumran [see "Resurrecting Scripture: The Discovery of the Dead Sea Scrolls" on page 61] tells us much about a group of people that the New Testament ignores.

BW: The thing that excites me the most about biblical archaeology is discovering archaeological findings that illuminate and authenticate the biblical text.

What is a typical dig day like?

BW: Because of the warm temperatures encountered in Bible lands, excavation work on a dig site is usually carried out between sunup and midday. After returning to the dig headquarters, all dig volunteers help wash the pottery recovered in the morning's digging. While this is going on, the staff archaeologists examine the pottery from the previous day's digging. They date the pottery and determine which pottery should be saved for further processing. Other dig staff members may be involved in registering objects and saved pottery, drawing pottery, completing dig records, and so on, during this time. The afternoon work period is usually followed by an hour or two of free time until supper. Following supper there is normally a lecture by one of the staff archaeologists. Attendance is required for students obtaining credit for participating in the dig and optional for other volunteers.

TB: You usually are excavating by six o'clock in the morning, in order to take advantage of the cooler part of the day and to finish work shortly after noon. You have "first breakfast" before the excavation begins, and a more substantial "second breakfast" midmorning. Lunch is usually held after the excavation concludes around one o'clock in the afternoon. After time for a shower and a short nap, pottery washing and reading occupies the late afternoon. Oftentimes after supper, there is a lecture related to the excavation.

What is the most significant find you've made? And why is it important?

BW: The most significant find I have made in my career was the discovery of Joshua's Ai (Joshua 7–8) at the site of Khirbet el-Maqatir, ten miles north of Jerusalem. It is significant because archaeologists had previously claimed that Joshua's Ai was located at et-Tell, six-tenths of a mile east of Kh. el-Maqatir, where there is no evidence for occupation at the time of Joshua. This led scholars to conclude that the biblical account of the capture of Ai by the Israelites in Joshua 7–8 is not historical. At Kh. el-Maqatir, on the other hand, the Associates for Biblical Research excavation from 1995 to 2000 discovered a small fortress from the time of Joshua which meets all of the biblical requirements to be identified as Joshua's Ai.

For biblical archaeology, what, in your opinion, is the most important find ever made? Why?

TB: Undoubtedly, the most important archaeological discovery is the Dead Sea Scrolls.

BW: Most scholars agree that the most important discovery related to the Bible is the parchment manuscripts found in the vicinity of Qumran on the west side of the Dead Sea, commonly referred to as the Dead Sea Scrolls. It is a rare find because parchment would normally not survive the damp conditions in this part of the world. Because the manuscripts were hidden in about AD 68 in caves near the Dead Sea, where it is extremely dry, they survived to be discovered in 1947. The reason this discovery is so important is that many of the scrolls are biblical texts of the Old Testament dating a thousand years before our previously oldest manuscripts. They demonstrate that our Old Testament was accurately transmitted during this thousand-year period.

How do you determine the date of an object?

TB: Most objects are not intrinsically datable, and so we rely on datable objects found in the same context. But since intrinsically datable objects (like inscriptions) are rare, archaeologists have developed a refined pottery typology, which takes advantage of the reality that pottery styles changed over time. Because everyone in the ancient world used pottery vessels, pottery sherds are everywhere, and archaeologists use these to determine all material found in the same context as these pottery sherds.

BW: For areas such as Mesopotamia, Turkey, Syria, and Egypt, where ancient inscriptions are common, inscriptions often provide information that can be used for dating. The most common method for dating objects found in Israel and Jordan, where ancient inscriptions are rare, is to date the pottery found in association with the object. For time periods after the introduction of coinage, coins are an accurate means of determining dates since they are normally inscribed with the year of a ruler. Other less-used, and often less-accurate, methods include carbon 14 dating, dating by style or material of the object, and dating by style or material of other material culture items found in association with the object.

What can archaeology prove or teach us about the Bible? What are its limitations?

BW: Archaeological findings have revolutionized our understanding of the Bible. Through the discoveries of archaeology, we have ancient texts that help us better understand the original languages of the Bible as well as the world of the Bible. The people, places, history, religion, and material culture of the Bible are much better understood as a result of archaeological finds. Many finds are limited in that they are "silent" and have to be interpreted. This leads to a variety of understandings by various scholars.

TB: Archaeology illuminates the world of the Bible. The Bible was written to a contemporary audience, who didn't need an explanation of what a house looked like, how a city gate functioned, or what types of tombs people were buried in. Its original readers knew all of this and much more. But today we live in a different world and culture, and archaeology helps to bridge the gap so that we can more properly understand the context in which the Bible was written. Archaeology cannot prove the Bible as a whole, but it can support and confirm the Bible's records of events. Some people today think that the Bible was a myth written hundreds of years after the events it purports to describe, but archaeological evidence reveals the names of people and places that confirm that the Scriptures were written by firsthand witnesses. Archaeology cannot prove many aspects of the text, such as the faith of the people or the supernatural work of God. Furthermore, archaeology has a significant weakness: all discoveries are subject to a human interpreter, who is fallible. Many archaeological discoveries have been misinterpreted, both by those who believe the Scriptures and by those who deny them. This is the nature of the discipline of archaeology, and believers should not place too much confidence in the discoveries of archaeology per se because of the ambiguity involved in much of the evidence.

Todd Bolen overlooking the Jezreel Valley

What role does faith play within the scientific discipline of archaeology?

TB: Archaeology should not be carried out in order to prove some pre-conceived idea, whether pro- or anti-Bible. Archaeology is best when it is carried out with the best of scientific methods and interpreted by a range of scholars. Archaeology is ill-served when the interpretation of sites and artifacts is divorced from our knowledge of ancient texts, including the Bible.

BW: Faith plays a significant role in interpreting archaeological finds related to the Bible in that it influences a scholar's presuppositions. Many scholars approach the Bible with the idea that it is a religious book and therefore contains exaggerated or contrived accounts to support the religious message of the Book. Such an individual will only accept the statements of the Bible if those statements can be backed up by evidence from outside the Bible. Thus, according to this view, the Bible is "guilty until proven innocent." A person of faith who accepts the validity of the biblical text, on the other hand, will use the Bible as a valid historical source which can be used to interpret the findings of archaeology.

Has archaeology revealed anything that contradicts the Bible? If so, what? And how should Christians respond to such discoveries?

BW: There are a number of supposed disagreements between the findings of archaeology and the Bible. In each case, however, the supposed disagreement involves a scholar's superficial and erroneous *interpretation* of an archaeological find rather than an objective fact. When an in-depth analysis is done of the so-called disagreement, it is found that, when properly interpreted, the archaeological find fully supports the accuracy of the Bible.

TB: Archaeology has revealed many things that can be interpreted in a fashion that is not compatible with the biblical record. But those same things can also be interpreted in a way that is consistent with Scripture. This ambiguity is not intrinsic to issues related to faith, but is the nature of the discipline. But those matters related to the Bible are naturally more popular and receive more attention in the press. I do not know of any major issues that conflict with the accuracy of the Bible. There are some issues of a lesser nature that are not yet resolved, but I recognize that that is due to the limited nature of the evidence.

What haven't we asked that is important for our readers to know?

TB: No archaeologists are unbiased. This is something that the public doesn't know when an archaeological story is covered. Some archaeologists are able to interpret any discovery in a way that appears to go against the biblical record. A few archaeologists may suggest a biblical connection when such is unlikely. Archaeologists are real people with real pasts. Few of them are people of faith, and some of them work in reaction to the faith of others. But when an archaeologist is interviewed in a magazine or on television, the public usually does not know the personal history of the individual or his or her record of interpretations. But this can be very important in properly assessing the credibility of the archaeologist.

BW: It is important to know how pottery, the basis for dating in Palestinian archaeology, was originally dated. Pottery as a means of dating is especially important for the Old Testament period. For the intertestamental period [the four hundred years between the Testaments] and New Testament period, coins provide the best means of dating. Pottery has several characteristics which make it very useful to the archaeologist. First is its durability. Because pottery is kiln-fired, it is rock-hard and virtually indestructible. Although an ancient pottery vessel can be broken into pieces (potsherds or sherds), those pieces will survive to be discovered by the archaeologist thousands of years later. Second, as with all things man-made, pottery changes through time—its shape, method of manufacture, decoration, and so on.

The Old Testament period is divided into various archaeological periods: Early Bronze Age, Middle Bronze Age, Late Bronze Age, and Iron Age. These major periods are further divided into subperiods. Each archaeological period has distinctive material cultural traits, including the type of pottery in use. For the pre-kingdom period of Old Testament history (Bronze Age and early part of the Iron Age), the various archaeological phases are dated by means of Egyptian inscriptions containing the names of Egyptian kings that have been found in Palestine. Because a detailed chronology has been worked out for Egyptian history, the archaeological phases, and in turn the pottery associated with each phase, can be dated.

For the kingdom period of Old Testament history (later part of the Iron Age), it is possible to correlate the archaeological phases with particular Israelite kings, based on historical information given in the Bible. Because the dates of the Israelite kings are known as a result of synchronisms (connections) with Assyrian and Babylonian history, the kingdom period archaeological phases, and in turn the pottery associated with each phase, can be dated.

* * *

We may never thrill at Bryant Wood or Todd Bolen cracking a bullwhip or outrunning a giant boulder in the movies. And though the work they do in the dirt and in the classroom seems tedious, it is more significant than any celluloid archaeologist's heroics. Because of their dedication to the Bible and the exacting work of archaeology, we gain a better perspective and appreciation of the people, places, and events recorded in God's Word. Now, what could be more exciting than that?

RESURRECTING SCRIPTURE
The Discovery of the Dead Sea Scrolls

by Wayne Stiles

Our guide pointed from the road to a rocky outcropping in the distant hills.

"This hike is definitely optional," he warned us. "But it's worth it."

A few of us brave souls followed, and for the first time in my life, I wished I had four legs. The quarter-mile climb between the bus and the hills proved to be the hardest of the hikes I took in Israel. The loose rocks over which I toddled were large, hot, and pointed. I had to calculate every step. There was no enjoying the view. Our guide scurried over the rocks like a lizard and stopped halfway up the hill, near the fissure in the rocks to which he had pointed. He turned and stood, arms crossed, one leg over the other, and waited for us. Finally, I arrived.

"This is it," he beamed.

Still panting, I entered the small cave which inside looked about the size of a spare bedroom. Empty . . . but bursting with significance. The contrast between the crudity of the cave and the profundity of its history still staggers me.

In 1947, the same year that the United Nations voted to establish a Jewish state in Palestine, a Bedouin shepherd tossed a rock in this cave, allegedly looking for a lost sheep. Why—or how—a sheep would ever wander up here makes no sense. Our guide told us that the Bedouin more likely was a looter in sheep's clothing who fabricated the whole affair to legitimize his discovery. Regardless, what he found in the cave made biblical history—or rather, I should say, confirmed it.

I turned around and looked out of the cave at the Dead Sea below me. In this area, called Qumran, just south of where Jesus was baptized—and during the same century—a small Essene community scribbled away copies of the Scriptures and other texts. They sealed their scrolls in clay jars and hid them in caves near the shores of the nearby Dead Sea—the place from which these now famous scrolls received their name. I stood in "Cave 1," so called because it was found first.

The view out of Qumran's "Cave 1" toward the Dead Sea

Significance of the Scrolls

Prior to the discovery of the Dead Sea Scrolls, scholars despaired of ever finding Hebrew manuscripts that predated our oldest copies from the tenth century AD. The manuscripts found at Qumran, however, dated from the third century BC to AD 70 and included copies of every Old Testament book except Esther. In other words, this discovery moved back our understanding of the text of the Hebrew Bible by about *one thousand years*! Comparing the biblical scrolls to the standard Hebrew Masoretic text has proven the remarkable precision in the copying of Scripture. In other words, the Hebrew Old Testament we read today is the same one Jesus read.

Eleven caves at Qumran have produced literally thousands of fragments and hundreds of scrolls from various literary works. From these extrabiblical writings we can better understand the culture in which Jesus lived, including its customs, traditions, theology, and concepts of the

Messiah. Both the biblical and extrabiblical writings found in the Qumran caves since 1947 continue to provide historians with vivid colors to fill in a once-gray sketch of religious life in the first century.

In the Light of God's Word

In Jerusalem today stands the Shrine of the Book, a museum that houses and displays many of the Dead Sea Scrolls. The shrine's massive white roof, shaped like the lid of one of the clay jars in which the scrolls were found, stands opposite a large, black wall of granite. The contrasting colors represent the "sons of light" and the "sons of darkness" and imply a principle: God's Word represents the difference between light and darkness (see Psalm 119:105; 2 Peter 1:19).

The Shrine of the Book museum in Jerusalem, which houses the Dead Sea Scrolls

Jesus revealed that it takes more than having God's Word to walk in the light. It takes belief in and obedience to His Word . . . even when the darkest of times tempt us to doubt. And they will.

In a book published just before the discovery, Frederic G. Kenyon wrote despairingly: "There is, indeed, no probability that we shall ever find manuscripts of the Hebrew text going back to a period before the formation of the text which we know as Massoretic [*sic*]. We can only arrive at an idea of it by a study of the earliest translations made from it."[1] Only eight years later, however, the Dead Sea Scrolls were discovered.

Isn't this often how we view life? All seems utterly hopeless, and then God steps in. Any one of us could have written something similar to Kenyon's quote about any situation. Conditions will often seem hopeless—*most* often, actually. Outcomes and attitudes will appear unchangeable and demand we doubt God's Word.

God can verify the reliability of Scripture and offer hope by many means, whether by resurrecting ancient manuscripts from the caves of Qumran . . . or by raising His Son from the cave that was His tomb.

But the task of believing and living His Word, God gives as our responsibility . . . and our privilege.[2]

A section of the Dead Sea Scrolls

*A facsimile of the entire Isaiah Scroll on display inside
The Shrine of the Book museum*

DIG THIS!

The Unity of Isaiah in the Dead Sea Scrolls

For years, critics had claimed the book of Isaiah had two authors—one who wrote the first thirty-nine chapters, and another who finished it much later. This claim stemmed from the fact that the two sections had different themes: judgment and comfort. The latter section also included fulfilled prophecies so accurate that liberal scholars claimed the text must have been penned after the fact.

But the discovery of the Dead Sea Scrolls at Qumran frustrated this theory. Today the Shrine of the Book in Jerusalem displays a facsimile of the entire scroll of Isaiah (see page 65). A glance at the text reveals no break between chapters 39 and 40. In fact, chapter 40 begins at the bottom of a column—clearly showing the unity of Isaiah.

Prior to the beginning of chapter 40, the scribe had made several errors—for instance, omitting an entire line he had to reinsert! If the scribe hadn't made that error, chapter 40 would have come at the start of a new column, giving the possible impression that it stands separate from the previous chapters. But the mistake kept the sections unified . . . just as Isaiah wrote them. This stands as one example of how God can use our flawed efforts to glorify Himself.

In the Judean Wilderness where the scrolls were discovered, the grass lives a very short time. Isaiah used this fact to illustrate what the discovery of the Dead Sea Scrolls supports: "The grass withers, the flower fades, / But the word of our God stands forever" (Isaiah 40:8).[1]

ABANDONED SHIP
A Sea of Galilee Boat Resurfaces

by Wayne Stiles

I could smell the fish before I saw them. Dirty boats with tackle and cranes floated on the Sea of Galilee while moored to the docks at En Gev. A fisherman stood knee-deep in fish, shoveling spadefuls onto a vertical conveyor belt that hauled buckets of sardines, musht, and barbels up to the awaiting ice.

Our tour group meandered down to the docks. We boarded a bulky boat made entirely of wood with "Matthew" sloppily painted on the hull. The sailors pulled in the tires that cushioned the vessel from the dock, and we shoved off.

As we sailed on the Sea of Galilee (really, a large lake), I stood at the bow and leaned over the edge, looking at the dark green water that parted against the keel below me. The boat slowed off the north shore.

A modern-day boat on the Sea of Galilee

Spring water flowed from a large pipe beside the place where the Jordan River empties into the lake. The springs attract fish to this part of the sea—and have for thousands of years. In fact, a fisherman stood on the shore holding his nets. At the sight of him, I tried to imagine the scene that took place here so long ago.

Simon Peter stood on the shore with his partners, James and John, cleaning their nets after a fruitless night of fishing. Jesus selected Peter's boat and taught the people from the lake. Afterward, Jesus turned to Peter.

"Put out into the deep water and let down your nets for a catch" (Luke 5:4). Reluctantly, Peter did so—at a location somewhere near where our boat was floating. The resulting catch produced enough fish to begin sinking two boats; that's a lot of fish!

On the shore, a dumbfounded Peter fell at Jesus's feet, fish still flopping all around them, and confessed: "Go away from me Lord, for I am a sinful man!" (5:8).

Jesus's response to Peter must have seemed as miraculous as the catch: "Do not fear, from now on you will be catching men" (Luke 5:10). The disciples left everything and followed Jesus.

The Discovery of a Boat from Jesus's Time

During a drought in 1986, two men, brothers like James and John, sons of a fisherman, were walking along the shores of the Sea of Galilee where they grew up. The water had receded lower than it had in years. Looking down, one brother saw an old nail in the mud, then another, and another. Then they unearthed some ancient wood. Unknowingly, they had discovered a boat from the time of Christ. Some would sensationally dub it "The Jesus Boat."

To excavate the vessel, archaeologists dug a trench around the remains of the boat while spraying water on the ancient wood to keep it moist. They braced the craft with fiberglass and applied a polyurethane spray that hardened around the frame, offering support. Once the boat became stable, the archaeologists flooded the trench and floated the boat to shore.

Over the next several years, scientists carefully infused synthetic wax into the wood, preserving it from any further deterioration and allowing it to survive when exposed to air. By comparing the manner of construction, analyzing nearby pottery vessels, and performing carbon 14 dating, archaeologists determined that the boat dates to between 100 BC and AD 70[1]—a range that includes the life of Christ.

Our group made its way to the Yigal Allon Museum at Nof Ginossaur, which displays the preserved first-century boat the brothers found. As we entered, a small, glass case displayed a scale model of the boat. "People were a lot smaller back then," someone joked.

The boat itself was marvelous. Made of oak and cedars of Lebanon, built with mortise-and-tenon joinery, the seven- by twenty-six-foot vessel could have held up to fifteen men.[2] Jesus and His disciples could have ridden in such a craft—a marvel to imagine.

The ancient, first-century boat on display

On one such occasion, after the miraculous feeding of the five thousand, Jesus put the disciples in a boat and pointed them across the lake (Mark 6:45). While Jesus remained alone on land praying, a storm arose on the water. The Sea of Galilee remains notorious for unexpected storms—even today. A squall in March of 1992 sent ten-foot-high waves crashing into downtown Tiberias, causing significant damage. Imagine the panicked "sinking feeling" of the disciples riding swells that high in a small boat this size!

Sometime between three and six a.m., Jesus came to the disciples by walking on the sea (Mark 6:48). But instead of expecting to see their miracle-working Lord, the dozen on board assumed Jesus was, of all things, a ghost! Jesus comforted them in reply, got into the boat, and stilled the storm. Then Mark wrote what has always seemed an unusual line to me: "They were utterly astonished, for they had not gained any insight from the incident of the loaves, but their heart was hardened" (6:51–52). What did the loaves have to do with the lake?

Lingering Lessons from the Lake

Academic tests determine how much information we know. But God's tests reveal how much information we apply. Jesus intended that the lesson of multiplying the loaves for the multitudes would get applied on the lake. His lecture had a lab. In both instances, the disciples' own attempts to do what Jesus commanded proved futile; they had to learn to depend upon Him for the impossible tasks (see Mark 10:27).

"Their heart was hardened," Mark wrote—as if the disciples had one heart. These men didn't expect Jesus to teach them about their inadequacy and dependency. Jesus had chosen the Twelve from out of all the multitudes who followed Him. They felt special. And as such, they

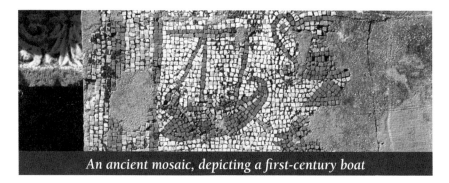

An ancient mosaic, depicting a first-century boat

expected special treatment. The storm struck them as strange because they expected Christ to give them privileged places in His kingdom. They did not anticipate Christ assigning them struggles to change their hardened heart.

And even though the disciples often appear as dumb as stumps, do we, by knowing more than they did, exhibit a greater faith? If we're honest, I think we'll see we resemble these men. The unrealistic expectations they had, which Jesus revealed, we also cling to in abundance. We have *our* agenda on how best to "serve God." All other events—especially storms—just get in the way. In reality, we live and serve with as much control as the disciples had in their foundering first-century boat.

Whenever I see the first-century boat on display or in photos, it reminds me that God's lectures and labs go together. Knowledge serves no purpose without the will and heart to obey.[3]

BATHED IN LIVING WATER
The Pool of Siloam

by John Adair

At 7 years old, my heart nearly jumped out of my chest. My over-worked stomach turned in endless rounds of somersaults. I stared down at the glimmering waters and wondered what they had in store for me. I'd been to the pool many times before. I adored the water. Our teacher had taught us the basics of getting around in the pool. I knew how to swim. I could tread water. We had even jumped off the diving board before. But today was diving day. Today would be different. Today I would lead with my head and open myself to that most shameful and painful of possibilities—the belly flop.

There the waters sat, awaiting my arrival. Time was short and the pressure was on . . . I dove. That half-second before impact lasted for an eternity. I waited for the impact, positioning myself for the best possible outcome. Splash! Into the water I sank, eventually rising to the top with feelings of elation and victory. It had worked! Pride swelled with the realization that I had avoided humiliation and completed the dive. My hopes for success were realized.

A Miraculous Healing

Rewind about two thousand years. A man tears through the streets of Jerusalem as quickly as his darkened vision will allow. He knows these streets by heart, down to the very step, a reality his blindness has forced him to accept. Today though, brimming over with a nervous energy similar to my own at the pool, he occasionally loses his place. In his haste, he takes a few corners too quickly and needs some redirection from bystanders. Everyone knows him—born blind and raised in this neighborhood. Some help him when they can, but most stare in puzzled silence at his excitable nature and dingy face.

This day will change his life forever. He had been approached by a man named Jesus, a man who claimed to heal the sick and make the blind see. Jesus had been walking by, discussing the spiritual causes of blindness when He stooped before the blind man, spit in the dirt, and placed the wet mixture on the man's eyes. Then Jesus told him to go and wash in the Pool of Siloam (John 9:1–7). So the blind man went. Quickly.

He finally arrives at the pool, standing with nervous energy before it. Would it work? How foolish would he look if it didn't? He throws himself toward the clean, clear waters, climbing down the plastered steps and into the pool, where he excitedly submerges himself.

Once under the water, he wipes the grimy mud from his eyes. Rising up from the pool with drops of water cascading down his face and neck, he opens his eyes. Joy and elation overwhelm him, and with the light pouring in to his renewed eyes, he catches a glimpse of just how much his life will change. He looks up to see the astonished faces of onlookers as he proclaims his sight. He runs home and sees his parents for the first time in his life—the people who have cared for him since infancy and have given all their energy to make sure he was provided for. And perhaps he harbors hopes of seeing the Man who had made all this possible.

Discovering the Pool

Such a significant moment in the life of this blind man healed by the power of Christ retains great interest for Christians today. To stand on the steps of the Pool of Siloam drives home the healing power of God in a unique way, even two thousand years later. In Jesus's time its location was obviously well-known, but by the fifth century, no one knew exactly where the pool was located, only that the water from Hezekiah's Tunnel should spill out into it. The empress Eudocia of Constantinople (AD 400–460) had a small pool and church constructed in a spot very near the entrance to the tunnel. This "upper" pool was rediscovered near the turn of the twentieth century, and up until recently, was the pool referred to when discussing the Pool of Siloam.[1]

However, it was clearly not the pool of Jesus's day, as that pool has since been rediscovered. In 2004, a construction team in Jerusalem

The "upper" pool, built in the fifth century AD

found a "lower" pool while digging up a sewer line in a small alleyway farther down the hill from the fifth-century pool. As the crew worked in the alley, some dirt fell away and two steps appeared. Construction was halted immediately, and when the excavation was completed, one entire side of the pool was exposed—more than 225 feet long!

This side of the pool has at least three sets of five limestone steps descending down into the water. The corners have been found at each end, revealing steps on at least three of the four sides of the pool. The corners are not exactly at right angles, indicating that the full pool was more of a trapezoid than a square or rectangle. However, the exact shape remains a mystery, because just beyond the excavated steps is a lush garden that is privately owned and, at this point, unavailable for exploration.

We can be sure of the dating of the pool based on several coins that were found at the site. These coins, some of which were pressed into the plaster bottom, date from the first century BC and the first century AD. This means that the pool would have been in use during Jesus's day, solidifying its connection to the healing of the blind man in John 9.[2]

As such, the Pool of Siloam, which constantly received fresh, running water from the Gihon Spring, remains a symbol of the living water that comes to humanity through Christ. We come into this world unclean and diseased, in need of a physician. And as He did for the blind man, Jesus offers healing and new life. We may tremble on the edge of the diving board, waiting to take the plunge.

But if we follow, we will find Him trustworthy as we are cleansed by the life-giving water He provides.

The "lower" pool of Jesus's day

ASCENDING THE HILL OF THE LORD
Exploring the Temple Mount

by Michael J. Svigel

At some points in the narrow tunnel, my shoulders scraped against the hewn stone, but my thick coat protected me not only from the rocks but from the subterranean cold. The long line of explorers snaked through the famous Western Wall Tunnel, retracing an ancient path that was once trodden by residents of Jerusalem passing by the famed Temple Mount.

As I watched my feet shuffle along the coarse stone floor below me, I suddenly bumped into the poor woman in front of me.

"Excuse me," I said.

"Traffic jam," she answered, looking ahead. The single-file line of tourists had slowed to a near stop. Cameras flashed, voices lowered to whispers, and gradually I approached the area that had drawn such attention. I expected to see a bottleneck in the tunnel, but instead the passageway widened where a sign marked the point in the Western Wall Tunnel that was closest to the ancient site of the Holy of Holies. Because of modern-day restrictions on non-Muslims visiting parts of the Temple Mount, this point was the nearest a Jew could get to the original site of the temple that had once been the center of Jewish faith and worship.

History of the Temple Mount

Solomon began construction on the first temple on Mount Moriah in Jerusalem in 966 BC (1 Kings 6:1–7). The beautiful structure was destroyed by the Babylonians in 586 BC (2 Kings 25:8–9). Like the mythical phoenix, the second temple rose from the ashes about seventy years later and was completed and consecrated by 515 BC under the leadership of Zerubbabel

(Ezra 6:15). Beginning in 20 BC, Herod the Great enlarged the Temple Mount to accommodate additional structures, reconstructing the temple structure itself. But in AD 70 the temple was destroyed by the Romans.[1]

In that second complex—built by Zerubbabel and expanded by Herod—Jesus and the apostles preached, taught, and performed miracles. In reference to Herod's magnificent structures, the disciples said to Jesus, "Teacher, behold what wonderful stones and what wonderful buildings!" To these exuberant words the Lord responded, "Do you see these great buildings? Not one stone will be left upon another which will not be torn down" (Mark 13:1–2).

After its violent destruction in AD 70, the Temple Mount has been a prize seized at different times by Roman governors, Jewish zealots, Muslim conquerors, and Christian crusaders. Even today, some parts of the Temple Mount are controlled by Jews, while others remain under the dominion of Muslims. Indeed, the story of the Temple Mount represents the violent history and extreme political and religious tensions that have engulfed the Holy Land for centuries.

A modern-day aerial view of the Temple Mount, with the same dimensions it had during Jesus's life

Excavating the Temple Mount

While the future of the Temple Mount is the stuff of prophetic specu-
lation, the site itself has long been the location of archaeological
excavations trying to uncover its rich and mysterious past. For more than
six centuries, the Temple Mount was virtually off-limits to non-Muslims,
and only a handful of westerners were granted limited access to visit
the intriguing locus of so many biblically significant places and events.
But in the late nineteenth century, European archaeologists were able to
conduct limited excavations that added to our overall understanding of
the Temple Mount. These legitimate archaeological pursuits were shut
down in 1911 after treasure seekers led by Montague Parker attempted
to find the Ark of the Covenant and Solomon's legendary treasures there.
Archaeologist Leen Ritmeyer recounts the fiasco:

> When Parker and his men entered the Dome of the Rock
> on the night of April 17th, a Muslim guard discovered
> their presence and the group had to flee Jerusalem, as
> the ensuing disturbances and rioting put their lives in
> danger. The sad result was that all exploration of the
> Temple Mount was prohibited until the Old City of
> Jerusalem was conquered by the Israelis in 1967.[2]

In 1968 excavations of the area around the Temple Mount began
in earnest, uncovering a wealth of archaeological information about the
Temple Mount and its environs. Several ancient gates and arches were
uncovered, matching historical accounts of this massive structure built
by Herod in his vast project to enlarge the Temple Mount to nearly twice
its original area. The results of these excavations include an expansion of
the area in front of the famous "Wailing Wall" as well as the Western Wall
Tunnel described at the beginning of this chapter. The Western Wall Tunnel
runs along the retaining wall built by Herod, which contains quarried
stones as large as twelve feet high, forty-five feet long, sixteen feet deep,
and weighing about five hundred tons![3]

On the southwest corner of the Temple Mount, archaeologists have
uncovered the remains of a stone-paved street that ran along the Western
Wall and continued along the Southern Wall. The street was damaged

when giant stones were thrown from the Temple Mount during the destruction of the temple in AD 70—a fulfillment of Christ's prophecy in Mark 13:2. Some of these stones are still visible, piled in a heap at the foot of the looming retaining wall.

Stones the Romans hurled from the temple above, crushing the first-century street

Not too far from this corner, near the center of the southern end of the Temple Mount, one finds the remains of a flight of stairs known today as the Southern Steps. Jesus and His followers would have walked on some of these very stones as they ascended the Temple Mount, and it may be that they passed by the foot of these steps as Christ led His disciples from the upper room to the Mount of Olives on the night of His betrayal.

Numerous volumes have been filled with the countless archaeological discoveries made on, around, and under the Temple Mount over the last century. This brief chapter could only mention a few of the impressive finds. Yet enough has been uncovered thus far to help us better understand the words of the disciples when they approached the city of Jerusalem more than two thousand years ago: "Behold what wonderful stones and what wonderful buildings!" (Mark 13:1).

DIG THIS!
The Resting Place of the
"Lost Ark of the Covenant"

Though the Ark of the Covenant played such a prominent role in the early history of Israel, its ultimate fate is shrouded in mystery. The instructions for building the ark are found in Exodus 25:10–22, and the last biblical mention of the ark's history is in 2 Chronicles 35:3. There it is described as resting in Solomon's temple, which was destroyed by the Babylonians in 586 BC.

Numerous legends, theories, and fictitious accounts have grown up around the mystery of the "lost ark." Some suggest it found its way to Axum, Ethiopia, where it is hidden to this day.[1] Some ancient Jewish sources suggest it is buried deep beneath the Temple Mount, still waiting to be discovered, while others say it was taken away and destroyed during the Babylonian invasion.[2] Some filmgoers may still be convinced that Indiana Jones found the ark in Egypt and packed it away in a vast government warehouse in the 1930s!

Regardless of where its final resting place may (or may not) be today, archaeologist Leen Ritmeyer may have found its original resting place in the Holy of Holies, a place still visible . . . at least to Muslims. His meticulous research and study of the present-day Temple Mount convinced him that the Holy of Holies of Solomon's temple and the original resting place of the Ark of the Covenant were situated on the actual "rock" section of the Muslim Dome of the Rock itself! In fact, a rectangular depression can still be seen on the surface of the rock, presumably the place where the Ark of the Covenant itself once rested![3]

"HE SUFFERED UNDER PONTIUS PILATE"
The Caesarean Inscription

by Michael J. Svigel

So You are a king?" the Roman prefect asked his prisoner (John 18:37). The question sounded more like ridicule than interrogation. The idea that this Jewish peasant was a king exceeded the bounds of sanity. *Where do the Jews get these ideas?*

The bruised and exhausted figure before him lifted his eyes slowly and met the stern gaze of the Roman prefect. With a voice barely above a mumble the prisoner answered, "You say correctly that I am a king. For this I have been born, and for this I have come into the world, to testify to the truth. Everyone who is of the truth hears My voice" (18:37).

The prefect frowned. *Truth . . . truth . . .* he thought. *If I hear another one of these Jews preach to me about truth. . . .* Sniffing indignantly, Pontius Pilate looked the Jew up and down and muttered partly to himself, "What is truth?" (18:38).

Though Pilate found "no guilt in" Jesus of Nazareth (18:38), he gave in to the demands of the frenzied crowd. To him Jesus was just another Jew—perhaps a bit overzealous, maybe misled, definitely out of touch with reality, but not a criminal like the murderer Barabbas. Nevertheless, the steps he took to appease the Jewish leaders would etch Pilate's name in history . . . and in the Christian faith.

Pontius Pilate in Scripture and History

Pontius Pilate, who reigned AD 26 to 36, is mentioned no less than fifty-six times in the New Testament as the governor of the Roman province of Judea that was caught up in the fury over Jesus of Nazareth. Though he symbolically "washed his hands" of the matter (Matthew 27:24), many key elements of the suffering, crucifixion, and burial of Christ occurred at his hands: the release of Barabbas in exchange for Jesus (27:17);

Jesus's scourging (Mark 15:15); the mob-inspired crucifixion
(John 19:15–16); the controversial inscription on the cross (John 19:19);
permission for Joseph of Arimathea to bury Jesus's body
(Matthew 27:57–58); and the guarding of the tomb (27:65). The saving
events of the gospel itself are intertwined with Pontius Pilate.

But what do we know of Pilate outside of these dramatic New Testament
accounts? Writing in the late first century, the Jewish historian Josephus
mentioned an incident in which Pilate, who dwelled in the port city
of Caesarea, set up in Jerusalem shields bearing images of Caesar. His
actions caused a crisis among the Jewish people because they viewed the
shields as reprehensible idols. In response to the Jews' passion for their
laws, Pilate eventually relented and removed the images.[1] In another
historical source from AD 109, the Roman historian Tacitus wrote,
"Christus . . . suffered the extreme penalty during the reign of Tiberius at
the hands of one of our procurators, Pontius Pilatus."[2]

Pontius Pilate in Archaeology

In 1961 an Italian team at the excavation site in Caesarea by the Sea
(where Pilate served as governor 1,900 years earlier) had been working
to unearth an ancient theater. One of the stones used to construct the
theater looked as if it had come from an earlier building, perhaps a temple or some other significant public building. On this stone, now worn,
the archaeologists read portions of a startling inscription in Latin:

[. . .]sTiberiévm

[pon]TivsPilaTvs

[praef]ecTvsivda[ea]e [3]

Though fragmented, the original content of the inscription is clear:
"Pontius Pilatus, Prefect of Judaea." This discovery marked significant
archaeological evidence substantiating the biblical and historical person
of Pontius Pilate and his office as prefect in the first century. One scholar
notes that the discovery of this inscription also helps paint a historical
picture of Pilate:

It is probable that Pilate occupied himself with major
projects . . . and left Jewish matters in the hands of
Caiaphas and his priestly colleagues. One might say that
Pilate was westward facing, toward the Mediterranean
and Rome, not eastward facing, toward Jerusalem.[4]

Such a portrait fits the biblical description of a provincial Roman
governor more concerned with pleasing the emperor and constructing
buildings than fussing with local fanatics . . . especially in Jerusalem,
where he seems to have felt less at home than in Caesarea. It is no
wonder, then, that Pilate deferred to the desires of the high priest's mob
in dealing with Jesus. Pilate was no weak-willed waffler; he just had no
patience for this kind of situation and would rather let the Jews handle
matters of religious "truth" themselves.

Replica of the Pontius Pilate Inscription at the ruins of Caesarea

Pontius Pilate in the Christian Creeds

Regardless of how many buildings were once inscribed with Pilate's
name, Pilate himself would be forever memorialized as the human agent
under whose purview the Lord of Glory was crucified. In AD 110, bishop
Ignatius of Antioch urged his readers that they have "full assurance in

regard to the birth, and passion, and resurrection which took place in the time of the government of Pontius Pilate."[5] Later in the second century, the Apostles' Creed—probably composed in Rome—declared as part of the baptismal confession that Jesus Christ was "born of the Virgin Mary, suffered under Pontius Pilate, was crucified, died, and was buried." And even at the Council of Nicaea, bishops from around the world declared the universal Christian faith, insisting that Jesus was "crucified also for us under Pontius Pilate."

Why has the church been so concerned with keeping Pontius Pilate's name as part of the very fabric of its beliefs? The answer is simple: *Christianity is a faith grounded in history, not mythology—in fact rather than fiction.* By declaring that Jesus of Nazareth died under the governorship of Pontius Pilate, Christians declare that the *historical* Jesus is the same as the Christ of faith. The death and resurrection of the God-man was a historical event tied to historical people, not a metaphorical or spiritual event tied merely to subjective faith.

The creeds that contain the name of Pontius Pilate are as historically real as the stone that bears the inscription, PONTIVSPILATVS. And therefore we can be confident in the inspired words of the apostle Peter:

> For we did not follow cleverly devised tales when we
> made known to you the power and coming of our Lord
> Jesus Christ, but we were eyewitnesses of His majesty.
> (2 Peter 1:16)

Ruins at the port of Caesarea

DIG THIS!
The Crucified Man from Giv'at ha-Mivtar

From the earliest days of the infant church, Christians preached about the crucifixion of Jesus Christ as the payment for our sins (Romans 5:8–9; 1 Corinthians 2:2). And for centuries, artwork, sculptures, and icons have depicted the crucifixion of the Son of God as a means of meditation on the price that was paid for our salvation.

While numerous historical documents mention the Roman practice of crucifixion, archaeologists had not discovered any evidence of the practice until 1968 when the remains of a man who died by crucifixion were found in a burial cave in Israel.[1] What is most astonishing about this discovery is that a nail used to affix the man to the cross was still lodged in the bones of the man's foot (see picture on page 88). In the process of studying the artifact, which even included fragments of wood from the cross, the original researchers drew the following initial conclusions:

> The feet were joined almost parallel, both trans-
> fixed by the same nail at the heels, with the legs
> adjacent; the knees were doubled, the right one
> overlapping the left; the trunk was contorted; the
> upper limbs were stretched out, each stabbed by a
> nail in the forearm.[2]

Later scholars reinterpreted the evidence and suggested the man had actually straddled the cross—with arms tied around the cross beam and each foot nailed to the right and left sides of the vertical post respectively.[3] In either case, this archaeological evidence of crucifixion corresponds quite closely to the images of Jesus's death on a cross—feet nailed to the post, arms outstretched in the "T" shape that has come to represent the saving work of Christ.

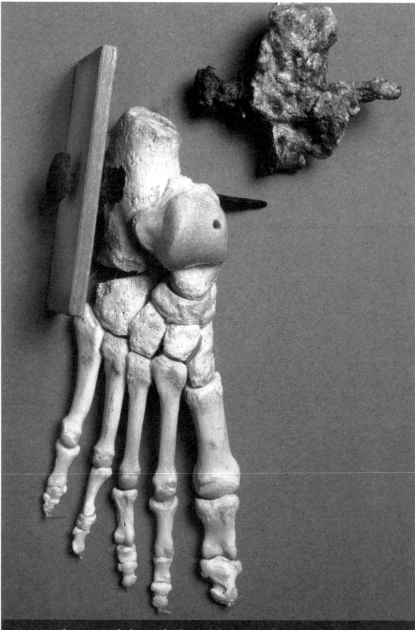

Above: Nail through the ankle bone of a crucified man
Below: Replica of a human foot, showing the placement of the nail

APPENDIX

GLOSSARY

Take a few minutes to familiarize yourself with some of the commonly used archaeological terms you'll find throughout this resource. Please note that the words in bold text are defined elsewhere in this glossary.

acropolis—Known as the "upper city"; the highest part of an ancient Greek city where all of the important buildings would be, such as temples and palaces

amphora (pl. **amphorae**)—A two-handled pottery vessel used for the storage of commodities such as wine, oil, water, and grain

ashlar masonry—Finished **square** blocks of building stone

balk—A one-meter-wide strip of earth left standing between excavation **squares**; provides both a walkway and a vertical cross-section of the archaeological and natural layers of the excavation **square**

casemate wall—A double city wall with a narrow space divided by transverse partitions into small chambers; sometimes used as rooms and sometimes filled with earth and stones to strengthen the wall

Cyclopean masonry—Walls comprised of very large uncut stones interspersed with smaller stones and rubble; or a partly finished wall of large close-fitting irregular stones

diagnostic sherd—A handle, base, rim, decoration, or other unique part of an ancient clay vessel that is useful for dating

dump—An area where the excavation director has determined that dirt removed from the excavation **squares** should be placed

glacis—A sloping, earthen embankment surrounding an ancient city which formed part of the fortification system

grid—A numbered pattern of lines laid out across the plan of a site; usually, but not always, running north-south and east-west over the area that is to be excavated

in situ—A Latin term meaning "in place"; referring to finding something in its original position

khirbet—An Arabic term meaning "ruin"; normally referring to a site which does not have a significant build-up of ancient debris forming a mound (see *tell*)

level—Refers to the height above sea level or a known datum point of an archaeological feature such as a wall, floor, artifact, and so on

locus—A three-dimensional, definable, man-made, or natural feature encountered during an excavation and given a number by the archaeologist; for example: walls, floors, ovens, pits, ash layers, different colored soils, and so on

necropolis—Literally meaning "city of the dead"; an ancient cemetery or burial ground

orthostat—An upright, finished stone slab forming part of a wall or doorway

ostracon (pl. **ostraca**)—A broken piece of pottery that includes writing in ink

potsherd—A broken piece of pottery

probe—A small exploratory pit or trench that is excavated to clarify the nature of underlying deposits

provenance—The origin or source of something

sarcophagus—A coffin of stone, clay, metal, or wood in which the ancients placed their dead for burial

sherd—A shortened form of **potsherd**

sounding—The same function as a **probe**, but usually of a larger size; archaeologists may make a "sounding" down to the level of bedrock to determine which historical periods are present at a particular site

square—A predetermined area where an excavation will take place, typically five meters by five meters in size, positioned with the site **grid** system; archaeologists usually supervise the excavation of the **square** and keep necessary records; other members of the team are responsible for digging, removing the dirt to a **dump** area, assisting with taking measurements, obtaining levels, and so on

stela or **stele**—An upright stone slab with a carved inscription

stratification—Superimposed occupational layers of an ancient site

stratigraphic method—The practice of excavating an ancient site one occupational layer at a time; identifying all features associated with that layer and carefully recording all finds as they are uncovered

stratigraphy—The process of observing, recording, reconstructing, and interpreting the **stratification** of a site

stratum—A definable occupation layer of a site representing one historical and cultural period; usually given a Roman numeral starting with *I* at the highest **stratum** and continuing down to the lowest layer

tabun—An Arabic term for a beehive-shaped oven made of clay; usually with large **sherds** pressed into its outer surface

tel—A Hebrew term for *tell*

tell—An Arabic term for an artificial mound built up by an accumulation of occupational debris which marks the site of an ancient city; in Israel, the shape of many tells is caused by an earthen embankment (**glacis**) defensive system built during the Middle Bronze Age; sometimes spelled "tall"; equivalent to Persian *tepe* and Turkish *hüyük*

tumulus—An artificial mound of earth covering a tomb

Commonly Used Tools at a Dig Site

brush—For cleaning walls and other areas to clarify what has been found; also used to prepare an artifact or area for a photo

dustpan—For collecting small amounts of soil to place in a **guffah**

guffah—A rubber container with handles made from an old automobile tire; used to collect soil from an excavation area and remove it from the **square**

hand broom—For cleaning walls and other areas to clarify what has been found; also used to prepare an artifact or area for a photo

hand pick—A small, hand-held pick used for the majority of excavating work in the **square**

large hoe—Used to scrape excavated soil into a **guffah**

large pick—For initially loosening the soil before carefully removing it by hand excavation

pottery bucket—A plastic bucket in which pottery **sherds** recovered during the excavation are placed; the archaeologist must label the bucket with the necessary information to determine where the **sherds** came from in the excavation **square**, including date, **square** number, **locus** number, and **pottery bucket** number; great care must be exercised not to mix pottery coming from different parts of the **square**; i.e., the excavators must ensure that the pottery they are excavating is placed in the correct bucket

sieve—Used to sift soil from an area (such as a tomb) where it is suspected that there might be small items that could escape the attention of excavators during hand excavation

small digging tools—For delicate work such as excavating a fragile artifact or skeletal remains in a tomb; instruments used include dental picks, pocketknife blades, syringes, small paint **brushes**, and toothbrushes

theodolite—A precision survey instrument used to establish horizontal and vertical distances; with this instrument a plan of the site can be developed and the locations of **grid** lines and excavation **squares** can be established

trowel—Basic tool used in cleaning stones, scraping the soil to reveal features, scraping soil into a **dustpan** for removal from the **square**, and excavating small areas

wheelbarrow—Used to transport soil removed from the excavation **square** to the **dump** area

HOW TO BEGIN A RELATIONSHIP WITH GOD

Archaeology paints a fascinating picture of those who have come before us, illuminating history with engaging details. Biblical archaeology has uncovered so many artifacts that are directly related to events, people, or places mentioned in the Scriptures. The discovery of the Walls of Jericho or the Dead Sea Scrolls can suddenly shift our perspectives, changing what we've read before as "Bible stories" into recorded history.

The Bible is a true, real, historical book. And the God of the Bible is just as real. He deeply desires to know you. But how? The Bible highlights four essential truths to beginning a relationship with God. Let's look at each one in detail.

Our Spiritual Condition: Totally Depraved

The first truth is rather personal. One look in the mirror of Scripture, and our human condition becomes painfully clear:

> There is none righteous, not even one;
> There is none who understands,
> There is none who seeks for God;
> All have turned aside, together they have become
>   useless;
> There is none who does good,
> There is not even one. (Romans 3:10–12)

We are all sinners through and through—totally depraved. Now, that doesn't mean we've committed every atrocity known to humankind. We're not as *bad* as we can be, just as *bad off* as we can be. Sin colors all our thoughts, motives, words, and actions.

You still don't believe it? Look around. Everything around us bears the smudge marks of our sinful nature. In spite of our best efforts to create a perfect world, crime statistics continue to soar, divorce rates keep climbing, and families keep crumbling.

Something has gone terribly wrong in our society and in ourselves—something deadly. Contrary to how the world would repackage it, "me-first" living doesn't equal rugged individuality and freedom; it equals death. As Paul said in his letter to the Romans, "The wages of sin is death" (Romans 6:23)—our spiritual and physical death that comes from God's righteous judgment of our sin, along with all of the emotional and practical effects of this separation that we experience on a daily basis. This brings us to the second marker: God's character.

God's Character: Infinitely Holy

How can God judge each of us for a sinful state we were born into? Our total depravity is only half the answer. The other half is God's infinite holiness.

The fact that we know things are not as they should be points us to a standard of goodness beyond ourselves. Our sense of injustice in life on this side of eternity implies a perfect standard of justice beyond our reality. That standard and source is God Himself. And God's standard of holiness contrasts starkly with our sinful condition.

Scripture says that "God is Light, and in Him there is no darkness at all" (1 John 1:5). God is absolutely holy—which creates a problem for us. If He is so pure, how can we who are so impure relate to Him?

Perhaps we could try being better people, try to tilt the balance in favor of our good deeds, or seek out methods for self-improvement. Throughout history, people have attempted to live up to God's standard by keeping the Ten Commandments or living by their own code of ethics. Unfortunately, no one can come close to satisfying the demands of God's law. Romans 3:20 says, "By the works of the Law no flesh will be justified in His sight; for through the Law comes the knowledge of sin."

Our Need: A Substitute

So here we are, sinners by nature and sinners by choice, trying to pull ourselves up by our own bootstraps to attain a relationship with our holy Creator. But every time we try, we fall flat on our faces. We can't live a good enough life to make up for our sin, because God's standard isn't "good enough"—it's *perfection*. And we can't make amends for the offense our sin has created without dying for it.

Who can get us out of this mess?

If someone could live perfectly, honoring God's law, and would bear sin's death penalty for us—in our place—then we would be saved from our predicament. But is there such a person? Thankfully, yes!

Meet your substitute—*Jesus Christ*. He is the One who took death's place for you!

> [God] made [Jesus Christ] who knew no sin to be sin on our behalf, so that we might become the righteousness of God in Him. (2 Corinthians 5:21)

God's Provision: A Savior

God rescued us by sending His Son, Jesus, to die on the cross for our sins (1 John 4:9–10). Jesus was fully human and fully divine (John 1:1, 18), a truth that ensures His understanding of our weaknesses, His power to forgive, and His ability to bridge the gap between God and us (Romans 5:6–11). In short, we are "justified as a gift by His grace through the redemption which is in Christ Jesus" (3:24). Two words in this verse bear further explanation: *justified* and *redemption*.

Justification is God's act of mercy, in which He declares believing sinners righteous, while they are still in their sinning state. Justification doesn't mean that God *makes* us righteous, so that we never sin again, rather that He *declares* us righteous—much like a judge pardons a guilty criminal. Because Jesus took our sin upon Himself and suffered our judgment on the cross, God forgives our debt and proclaims us PARDONED.

Redemption is Christ's act of paying the price to release us from sin's bondage. God sent His Son to bear His wrath for all of our sins—past, present, and future (Romans 3:24–26; 2 Corinthians 5:21). In humble obedience, Christ willingly endured the shame of the cross for your sake (Mark 10:45; Romans 5:6–8; Philippians 2:8). Christ's death satisfied

God's righteous demands. He no longer holds your sins against you, because His own Son paid the penalty for them. You are freed from the slave market of death, never to be a slave again!

Placing Your Faith in Christ

These four truths describe how God has provided a way to Himself through Jesus Christ. Because the price has been paid in full by God, we must respond to His free gift of eternal life in total faith and confidence in Him to save us. We must step forward into the relationship with God that He has prepared for us—not by doing good works or by being a good person but by coming to Him just as we are and accepting His justification and redemption by faith.

> For by grace you have been saved through faith; and that not of yourselves, it is the gift of God; not as a result of works, so that no one may boast. (Ephesians 2:8–9)

We accept God's gift of salvation simply by placing our faith in Christ alone for the forgiveness of our sins. Would you like to enter a relationship with your Creator by trusting in Christ as your Savior? If so, here's a simple prayer you can use to express your faith:

> *Dear God,*
>
> *I know that my sin has put a barrier between You and me. Thank You for sending Your Son, Jesus, to die in my place. I trust in Jesus alone to forgive my sins, and I accept His gift of eternal life. I ask Jesus to be my personal Savior and the Lord of my life. Thank You. In Jesus's name, amen.*

If you've prayed this prayer or one like it and you wish to find out more about knowing God and His plan for you in the Bible, contact us at Insight for Living. You can speak to one of our pastors on staff by using the information below:

Pastoral Ministries Department
Insight for Living
Post Office Box 269000
Plano, Texas 75026-9000
(972) 473-5097, Monday through Friday
8:00 a.m. – 5:00 p.m. Central time
www.insight.org/contactapastor

WE ARE HERE FOR YOU

If you desire to find out more about knowing God and His plan for you in the Bible, contact us. Insight for Living provides staff pastors and women's counselors who are available for free written correspondence or phone consultation. These seminary-trained and seasoned men and women have years of pastoral experience and are well-qualified guides for your spiritual journey.

Please feel welcome to contact our Pastoral Ministries department by using the information below:

Insight for Living
Pastoral Ministries Department
Post Office Box 269000
Plano, Texas 75026-9000
(972) 473-5097, Monday through Friday,
8:00 a.m. – 5:00 p.m. Central time
www.insight.org/contactapastor

ENDNOTES

Introducing the *Real* Indiana Jones
Archaeologists and Their Work

1. Alfred Hoerth and John McRay, *Bible Archaeology: An Exploration of the History and Culture of Early Civilizations* (Grand Rapids: Baker Books, 2005), 10.

2. Hoerth and McRay, Bible *Archaeology*, 16. See also Joseph P. Free, *Archaeology and Bible History*, rev. and exp. Howard F. Vos (Grand Rapids: Zondervan, 1992), 17.

3. Hoerth and McRay, Bible Archaeology, 16–17, 18. See also Free, *Archaeology and Bible History*, 17, 19.

KEY OLD TESTAMENT FINDS

The Walls of Jericho
Physical Evidence of Supernatural Intervention

1. "Jericho," in *The New International Dictionary of Biblical Archaeology*, ed. Edward M. Blaiklock and R. K. Harrison (Grand Rapids: Zondervan, 1983), 258.

2. Alfred Hoerth and John McRay, *Bible Archaeology: An Exploration of the History and Culture of Early Civilizations* (Grand Rapids: Baker Books, 2005), 101.

3. "Jericho," ed. Blaiklock and Harrison, 258.

4. "Jericho," ed. Blaiklock and Harrison, 260.

5. Alan Millard, *Treasures from Bible Times* (Tring, Eng.: Lion, 1985), 96–97.

6. Joseph P. Free, *Archaeology and Bible History*, rev. and exp. Howard F. Vos (Grand Rapids: Zondervan, 1992), 112.

7.   Hoerth and McRay, *Bible Archaeology*, 108.

8.   "The Walls of Jericho," in *NIV Archaeological Study Bible: An Illustrated Walk through Biblical History and Culture*, ed. Walter C. Kaiser, Jr., and others (Grand Rapids: Zondervan, 2005), 312.

9.   Bryant Wood, "The Walls of Jericho," *Creation*, March 1999, www.answersingenesis.org/creation/v21/i2/jericho.asp, accessed January 14, 2008.

10. Free, *Archaeology and Bible History*, 111.

11. Free, *Archaeology and Bible History*, 109.

12. Wood, "The Walls of Jericho."

13. Wood, "The Walls of Jericho."

The Merneptah Stele
How *Not* to Date the Exodus

1.   Some scholars date Merneptah's reign from circa 1213–1203 BC, adjusting all previous pharaonic dates. Under this date, Merneptah's invasion of Canaan occurred in approximately 1210. It is difficult to be dogmatic about the times of the pharaohs' reigns, but the dating assumed in this article is based on Eugene H. Merrill, *Kingdom of Priests: A History of Old Testament Israel* (Grand Rapids: Baker Books, 1987), 58. His dating of the pharaohs corresponds nicely with the biblical record as outlined in this article.

2.   "The Merneptah Stele," in *NIV Archaeological Study Bible: An Illustrated Walk through Biblical History and Culture*, ed. Walter C. Kaiser, Jr., and others (Grand Rapids: Zondervan, 2005), 360.

3.   Alfred Hoerth and John McRay, *Bible Archaeology: An Exploration of the History and Culture of Early Civilizations* (Grand Rapids: Baker Books, 2005), 85.

4.   Alan Millard, *Treasures from Bible Times* (Tring, Eng.: Lion, 1985), 100–101.

5. Millard, *Treasures from Bible Times*, 100.

6. Millard, *Treasures from Bible Times*, 100.

7. "The Date of the Exodus," in *NIV Archaeological Study Bible*, 106. "Late date" proponents often cite Exodus 1:11 as evidence that the exodus happened during the reign of Rameses II because the Hebrews built storage cities for "Pharaoh," including "Raamses." There are compelling arguments as to why this reference is not to Rameses II, primarily that the use of the name Rameses did not originate with Rameses II, but much earlier, and the time period covering Exodus 1:11–12:42 (the building of the city through the exodus) is too long for Rameses II's reign. Eugene Merrill in *Kingdom of Priests* closely evaluates these arguments (see pages 70–71).

8. See Merrill, *Kingdom of Priests*, 62, 68–69, for additional arguments against the "late date" theory of the exodus.

9. Edwin R. Thiele, *The Mysterious Numbers of the Hebrew Kings* (Grand Rapids: Eerdmans, 1965), 28, referenced in Merrill, *Kingdom of Priests*, 67, note 24.

10. See Merrill, *Kingdom of Priests*, 68, for a more complete treatment of the 1446 dating of the exodus based on Jephthah's memorandum.

11. Merrill makes a compelling case for the animosity between Thutmose III and Moses: the two may have been close adopted relatives (with Hatshepsut, Thutmose III's stepmother, as Moses's adopted mother, see Exodus 2:5–10); and, as the elder, Moses may have been first in line to inherit the kingdom. Thus, we see Thutmose III's desire to kill Moses for an offense that likely would have been overlooked under different circumstances. See *Kingdom of Priests*, 60, 62.

12. "The Date of the Exodus," in *NIV Archaeological Study Bible*, 106.

13. "The Pharaoh of the Exodus," in *NIV Archaeological Study Bible*, 98.

Dig This!
The Rosetta Stone: From Art to Eloquence

1.   See W. S. LaSor, "Archeology of Egypt," in *The International Standard Bible Encyclopedia*, vol. 1, *A–D*, rev. illustrated ed., ed. Geoffrey W. Bromiley and others (Grand Rapids: Eerdmans, 1988), 249. Also see C. E. DeVries, "Rosetta Stone," in *The International Standard Bible Encyclopedia*, vol. 4, *Q–Z*, 237.

2.   LaSor, "Archeology of Egypt," 250.

3.   Alan Millard, *Treasures from Bible Times* (Tring, Eng.: Lion, 1985), 26.

4.   "The Rosetta Stone and the Deciphering of Hieroglyphs," in *NIV Archaeological Study Bible: An Illustrated Walk through Biblical History and Culture*, ed. Walter C. Kaiser, Jr., and others (Grand Rapids: Zondervan, 2005), 101.

5.   LaSor, "Archeology of Egypt," 250.

King David Vindicated
The Discovery of the Dan Stele and High Place

1.   Alfred Hoerth and John McRay, *Bible Archaeology: An Exploration of the History and Culture of Early Civilizations* (Grand Rapids: Baker Books, 2005), 121.

2.   Chapter adapted from Wayne Stiles, *Going Places with God: A Devotional Journey through the Lands of the Bible* (Ventura, Calif.: Regal, 2006), 110; and from Wayne Stiles, *Walking in the Footsteps of Jesus: A Journey through the Lands and Lessons of Christ* (Ventura, Calif.: Regal, 2008). Used by permission.

Deliver Us from Evil
The Story of Hezekiah's Tunnel

1.   Alan Millard, *Treasures from Bible Times* (Tring, Eng.: Lion, 1985), 126.

2.   Millard, *Treasures from Bible Times*, 124–25.

3.   Millard, *Treasures from Bible Times*, 126–27.

Dig This!
The Last Days of Judah: The Lachish Letters

1.   "The Lachish Ostraca," in *NIV Archaeological Study Bible: An Illustrated Walk Through Biblical History and Culture*, ed. Walter C. Kaiser, Jr., and others (Grand Rapids: Zondervan, 2005), 1252.

2.   Alan Millard, *Treasures from Bible Times* (Tring, Eng.: Lion, 1985), 130.

The Ketef Hinnom Amulets
Tiny Bits of History with Enormous Implications

1.   "Jerusalem in the Time of Jesus," in *NIV Archaeological Study Bible: An Illustrated Walk through Biblical History and Culture*, ed. Walter C. Kaiser, Jr., and others (Grand Rapids: Zondervan, 2005), map 10.

2.   "Tombs in Ancient Israel," in *NIV Archaeological Study Bible*, 376.

3.   Gabriel Barkay and others, "The Challenges of Ketef Hinnom: Using Advanced Technologies to Reclaim the Earliest Biblical Texts and Their Context," *Near Eastern Archaeology*, vol. 66, no. 4 (December 2003), 162–71.

4.   John Noble Wilford, "Solving a Riddle Written in Silver," *The New York Times*, September 28, 2004, www.nytimes.com/2004/09/28/science/28scro.html, accessed February 20, 2008.

5.   Barkay, "The Challenges of Ketef Hinnom," 170.

6.   "Amulet," in *The New International Dictionary of Biblical Archaeology*, ed. Edward M. Blaiklock and R. K. Harrison (Grand Rapids: Zondervan, 1983), 26.

7.   Barkay, "The Challenges of Ketef Hinnom," 170.

8.   Barkay, "The Challenges of Ketef Hinnom," 170.

9.   "The Ketef Hinnom Amulets," in *NIV Archaeological Study Bible*, 204.

KEY NEW TESTAMENT FINDS

Resurrecting Scripture
The Discovery of the Dead Sea Scrolls

1. Frederic Kenyon, *Our Bible and the Ancient Manuscripts*, 4th ed. (London: Eyre & Spottiswoode, 1939), 48.

2. Adapted from Wayne Stiles, *Walking in the Footsteps of Jesus: A Journey through the Lands and Lessons of Christ* (Ventura, Calif.: Regal, 2008). Used by permission.

Dig This!
The Unity of Isaiah in the Dead Sea Scrolls

1. Adapted from Wayne Stiles, *Going Places with God: A Devotional Journey through the Lands of the Bible* (Ventura, Calif.: Regal, 2006), 121. Used by permission.

Abandoned Ship
A Sea of Galilee Boat Resurfaces

1. Israel Ministry of Foreign Affairs, "Archeological Sites in Israel—The Roman Boat from the Sea of Galilee," July 29, 1998, http://www.mfa. gov.il, accessed January 28, 2008.

2. Alfred Hoerth and John McRay, *Bible Archaeology: An Exploration of the History and Culture of Early Civilizations* (Grand Rapids: Baker Books, 2005), 163.

3. Chapter adapted from Wayne Stiles, *Walking in the Footsteps of Jesus: A Journey through the Lands and Lessons of Christ* (Ventura, Calif.: Regal, 2008). Used by permission.

Bathed in Living Water
The Pool of Siloam

1. Hershel Shanks, "Where Jesus Cured the Blind Man." *Biblical Archaeology Review* 31 (2005): 18.

2. Shanks, "Where Jesus Cured the Blind Man," 20–21.

Ascending the Hill of the Lord
Exploring the Temple Mount

1. "Temple," in *The New International Dictionary of Biblical Archaeology*, ed. Edward M. Blaiklock and R. K. Harrison (Grand Rapids: Zondervan, 1983), 445–46.

2. Leen Ritmeyer, *The Quest: Revealing the Temple Mount in Jerusalem* (Jerusalem: Carta Jerusalem and The Lamb Foundation, 2006), 18.

3. Ritmeyer, *The Quest*, 32.

Dig This!
The Resting Place of the "Lost Ark of the Covenant"

1. Barry Hoberman, "The Ethiopian Legend of the Ark," *Biblical Archaeologist* 46.2 (Spring 1983): 113–14, electronic ed, accessed through www.jstor.org.

2. These opposing traditions are found in *The Talmud of Babylonia: An American Translation*, vol. V.B: *Yoma Chapters Three through Five*, trans. Jacob Neusner (Atlanta: Scholars Press, 1994), 102.

3. Leen Ritmeyer, "The Ark of the Covenant: Where It Stood in Solomon's Temple," *Biblical Archaeology Review* 22.1 (January/February 1996): 46–55, 70–72.

"He Suffered under Pontius Pilate"
The Caesarean Inscription

1. Josephus, *Antiquities of the Jews*, 18.55–59, in *The Works of Flavius Josephus*, electronic ed., accessed through BibleWorks. See also Josephus, *The Wars of the Jews*, 2.169–174, in *The Works of Flavius Josephus*, electronic ed., accessed through BibleWorks.

2. Tacitus, *Annals* 15.44, http://classics.mit.edu/Tacitus/annals.11.xv.html, accessed January 21, 2008.

3. Jerry Vardaman, "A New Inscription Which Mentions Pilate as 'Prefect,'" *Journal of Biblical Literature* 81, no. 1 (1962), 70, electronic ed., accessed through www.jstor.org. Letters in brackets indicate missing characters restored by scholars.

4.   Craig A. Evans, "Excavating Caiaphas, Pilate, and Simon of Cyrene: Assessing the Literary and Archaeological Evidence," in *Jesus and Archaeology*, ed. James H. Charlesworth (Grand Rapids: Eerdmans, 2006), 337.

5.   Ignatius, *Letter to the Magnesians* 11.1, in *Ante-Nicene Fathers*, ed. Alexander Roberts, James Donaldson, A. Cleveland Coxe, electronic ed., accessed through BibleWorks.

Dig This!
The Crucified Man from Giv'at ha-Mivtar

1.   N. Haas, "Anthropological Observations on the Skeletal Remains from Giv'at ha-Mivtar," *Israel Exploration Journal* 20.1, 2 (1970): 49–59.

2.   Haas, "Anthropological Observations on the Skeletal Remains from Giv'at ha-Mivtar," 58.

3.   Joseph Zias and Eliezer Sekeles, "The Crucified Man from Giv'at ha-Mivtar: A Reappraisal," *Israel Exploration Journal* 35 (1985): 22–26.

RESOURCES FOR
PROBING FURTHER

To further your study of biblical archaeology, we recommend the following resources. Of course, we cannot always endorse everything a writer or ministry says, so we encourage you to approach these and all other non-biblical resources with wisdom and discernment.

BiblePlaces. www.bibleplaces.com — Created by Professor Todd Bolen, this Web site is filled with beautiful photos and useful information pertaining to many archaeological, historical, and biblical sites throughout the Middle East.

Biblical Archaeology Review. www.bib-arch.org

Blaiklock, Edward M., and R. K. Harrison, eds. *The New International Dictionary of Biblical Archaeology*. Grand Rapids: Zondervan, 1983.

Free, Joseph P. *Archaeology and Bible History*. Rev. and exp. by Howard F. Vos. Grand Rapids: Zondervan, 1992.

Freedman, David N., ed. *The Anchor Bible Dictionary*. Vols. 1–6. New Haven, Conn.: Yale University Press, 1992.

Hoerth, Alfred, and John McRay. *Bible Archaeology: An Exploration of the History and Culture of Early Civilizations*. Grand Rapids: Baker Books, 2005.

Kaiser, Walter C., Jr., and others, eds. *NIV Archaeological Study Bible: An Illustrated Walk through Biblical History and Culture*. Grand Rapids: Zondervan, 2005.

Millard, Alan. *Nelson's Illustrated Wonders and Discoveries of the Bible*. Nashville: Thomas Nelson, 1997.

Reed, Jonathan L. *The HarperCollins Visual Guide to the New Testament: What Archaeology Reveals about the First Christians.* New York: HarperOne, 2007.

Ritmeyer, Leen. *The Quest: Revealing the Temple Mount in Jerusalem.* Jerusalem: Carta Jerusalem and The Lamb Foundation, 2006.

Rose Book of Bible and Christian History Time Lines: More than 6000 Years at a Glance. Torrance, Calif.: Rose, 2006.

Shanks, Hershel. *Jerusalem's Temple Mount: From Solomon to the Golden Dome.* New York: Continuum, 2007.

Stiles, Wayne. *Going Places with God: A Devotional Journey through the Lands of the Bible.* Ventura, Calif.: Regal, 2006.

Stiles, Wayne. *Walking in the Footsteps of Jesus: A Journey through the Lands and Lessons of Christ.* Ventura, Calif.: Regal, available September 2008.

ABOUT THE WRITERS

John Adair

John received his bachelor's degree from Criswell College and his master of theology degree from Dallas Theological Seminary, where he recently completed his Ph.D. in historical theology. He serves as a writer in the Creative Ministries department of Insight for Living. John, his wife, Laura, and their two children reside in Frisco, Texas.

Brianna Barrier Engeler

Brie is a magna cum laude graduate of Baylor University and holds a master's degree in biblical studies from Dallas Theological Seminary. As an experienced researcher, editor, and writer, she greatly enjoys the opportunity she has to teach biblical truth through the ministry of Insight for Living. Brie and her husband, Derrek, live in Frisco, Texas.

Derrick G. Jeter

A graduate of Dallas Theological Seminary with a master's degree in theology, Derrick's passion is to exhort believers to understand and apply the Scriptures and to engage unbelievers with the truth of Christ's death and resurrection. Derrick presently serves as a writer for Insight for Living. He lives in the Dallas area with his wife, Christy, and their five children.

Wayne Stiles

After serving in the pastorate for fourteen years, Wayne joined the staff at Insight for Living and currently serves as executive vice president and chief content officer. He received his master of theology and doctor of ministry degrees from Dallas Theological Seminary. Wayne and his wife, Cathy, have two teenage daughters.

Michael J. Svigel

Mike has been writing for Insight for Living since 2004. He is a graduate of Dallas Theological Seminary, where he received his master of theology in New Testament, completed his Ph.D. in theological studies, and now serves as an assistant professor. Mike lives in the Dallas area with his wife, Stephanie, and their three children.

ORDERING INFORMATION

If you would like to order additional copies of *Insight's Archaeology Handbook* or order other Insight for Living resources, please contact the office that serves you.

United States

Insight for Living
Post Office Box 269000
Plano, Texas 75026-9000
USA
1-800-772-8888
Monday through Thursday
7:00 a.m. – 9:00 p.m. and
Friday, 7:00 a.m. – 7:00 p.m. Central time
www.insight.org
www.insightworld.org

Canada

Insight for Living Canada
Post Office Box 2510
Vancouver, BC V6B 3W7
CANADA
1-800-663-7639
www.insightforliving.ca

Australia, New Zealand, and South Pacific

Insight for Living Australia
Post Office Box 1011
Bayswater, VIC 3153
AUSTRALIA
1 300 467 444
www.insight.asn.au

United Kingdom and Europe

Insight for Living United Kingdom
Post Office Box 348
Leatherhead
KT22 2DS
UNITED KINGDOM
0800 915 9364
www.insightforliving.org.uk

Other International Locations

International constituents may contact the U.S. office through our Web site (www.insightworld.org), mail queries, or by calling +1-972-473-5136.